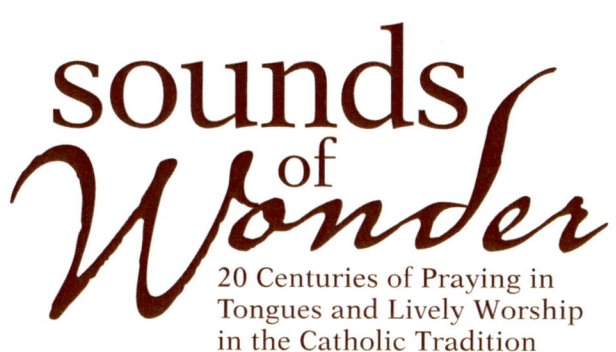

20 Centuries of Praying in Tongues and Lively Worship in the Catholic Tradition

Deacon Eddie Ensley, Ph.D.

Sounds of Wonder
20 Centuries of Praying in Tongues and Lively Worship
in the Catholic Tradition
Deacon Eddie Ensley, Ph.D.

Copyright © 2013, Eddie Ensley, All rights reserved.

Cover images: Shutterstock.com
Cover and book design: Tau Publishing Design Department

No part of this book may be reproduced, stored in a retrieval system or transmitted in any form or by any means - electronic, mechanical, photocopying, recording, or otherwise - without written permission of the publisher.

For information regarding permission, write to:
Tau Publishing, LLC
Attention: Permissions Dept.
4727 North 12th Street
Phoenix, AZ 85014

Paperback:
ISBN 978-1-61956-172-4
Hardcover:
ISBN 978-1-61956-183-0

Second Edition August 2013
10 9 8 7 6 5 4 3 2

Published and printed in the United States of America by Tau Publishing, LLC
For additional inspirational books visit us at TauPublishing.com

TauPublishing.com

Words of Inspiration

Endorsements

In this remarkable book Eddie Ensley opens up a whole new window into Catholic spirituality of the last two millennia. Ensley shows convincingly that the gift of tongues and other charismatic phenomena did not disappear from Christian tradition but continued in every age, especially in the form of jubilation, an exuberant prayer of the heart that overflows in wordless vocal praise. This book is a great resource for everyone interested in the charismatic dimension of the Church, which was, as John Paul II said, rediscovered at Vatican Council II.

—Mary Healy STD
Associate Professor of Sacred Scripture
at Sacred Heart Major Seminary,
Series Editor for Catholic Commentary on Sacred Scripture

"We absolutely need to recover an understanding and experience of all the workings of the Holy Spirit in order to have a maximally effective response to the Church's call for a new evangelization. Eddie Ensley's book is an important contribution."

—Ralph Martin STD
Associate Professor of Theology, Sacred Heart Major Seminary, appointed by the Pope as consultor to the Potifical Council for the New Evangelization

"*Sounds of Wonder*" is a gem of Catholic charismatic spirituality that I have often referred to in books and public presentations. It contains some evidence of the use of charismatic gifts and praise from the early Patristic era not often found elsewhere. I recommend it highly!

—John Michael Talbot, Christian musician, author of many books

For centuries after Paul and Luke, the Church prayed in tongues, even in the liturgy. They didn't call it tongues, they called it jubilation, though it scarcely differed from the way Paul describes the gift in First Corinthians. Thanks to Deacon Eddie Ensley's work we can now see this clearly. Having devoured his first edition, I heartily recommend this expanded second edition to all readers, especially bishops and pastors who have the office of fostering the charismatic gifts of the faithful.

—Father George Montague, SM
Professor of Theology, St. Mary's University, San Antonio,
Author of many books and scholarly studies.

Eddie Ensley's book, "Sounds of Wonder" has provided a clear understanding of the use of the Gift of Speaking in Tongues from the time of Pentecost to the present. This gift is an extraordinary gift of the Holy Spirit that is meant to be a normal prayer–expression of one who is filled with the Spirit. Deacon Ensley has carefully traced the use of this gift both in the life of individuals and in the life of communities in worship. He has taken his original book and has added many more references to the use of the Gift of Speaking in Tongues found in additional resources. In doing so, he has shown the richness in one's prayer life when a person is open to this and all the Gifts of the Holy Spirit. Deacon Ensley has once more provided a remarkable service through his research and insights into the wonder of the Holy Spirit through this gift.

—Bishop Samuel Jacobs
Bishop of Houma/Thibodaux

I welcome this reprint with update of Deacon Edie Ensley's study of the "Sounds of Wonder." It continues to be a call to learn from the Holy Spirit the wonders of praise and song. May this new edition be as helpful and encouraging as its predecessor and unlock for many the Spirit-given resources of praise.

—Fr. Francis Martin
Former Professor of New Testament,
Ecole Biblique, Jerusalem;
Domincan House of Studies,
Washington, DC,
author of *The Disclosure of the Word*

Dedication

This book is dedicated to Dominic Berardino M.A., Mary Healy, STD and Vinson Synan Ph.D., who strongly urged me to bring this book back into print and for Ralph Martin, STD who encouraged me to publish my research, nearly forty years ago.

Foreword
by Vinson Synan

It was in 1977 that I discovered Eddie Ensley's book *Sounds of Wonder: Speaking in Tongues in the Catholic Tradition*. For me it was an exciting eye opener to read about the story of speaking and singing in tongues through the centuries. Although written primarily for a Catholic audience, this book is really the story of how the gifts of the Spirit have been working in the church from the day of Pentecost to the present day. As such it is relevant to people of all church traditions, but especially for us in the Pentecostal tradition.

I not only devoured the book, but I have made it required reading in my classes on Pentecostal/Charismatic history to this day. Along with Kilian McDonnell and George Montague's groundbreaking research on the baptism in the Holy Spirit *Christian Initiation and the Baptism in the Holy Spirit: Evidence from the First Eight Centuries*, I have found from their research that Pentecostalism was at the heart of the Catholic public liturgy for many centuries. Therefore Pentecostalism is not something new but has been deeply embedded in the Church from the beginning.

Being also deeply interested in music, classical guitar has been my hobby for years, I was fascinated to learn that singing in tongues was the foundation of the Gregorian chant and eventually all notated music in the West. In time this singing in the Spirit was called jubilate. Ensley's descriptions and citations of Jubilate, or "wordless songs of praise," sound remarkably like "singing in the Spirit" that is so common in Pentecostal and Charismatic worship today. Prominent figures in the story are St. Augustine and St. Thomas Acquinas, both major Catholic theologians. I think that this explains why Catholics saw charismatic worship as profoundly rooted in their own church tradition and not necessarily an import from Protestantism.

Ensley writes as both a scholar and participant in the Catholic Charismatic renewal for many years. Despite physical handicaps that would have stymied lesser men, he overcame everything to earn a B.A. at Belhaven College, an M.A. degree from Loyola University, and a Ph.D. from Cornerstone University. After his baptism in the Holy Spirit with speaking in tongues he joined the prayer meeting in the home of Dr. Rodman Williams at Austin Presbyterian Theological Seminary in Texas. Although his spiritual formation was in the Presbyterian Church, as a youth he was drawn to the Roman Catholic Church and in 1972 he became a Roman Catholic. He was ordained a deacon in 2001.

It is now a blessing that Deacon Ensley has done more research and is now republishing *Sounds of Wonder* for a new generation of scholars and Spirit-filled believers. In this work he has added many more testimonies to jubilation and speaking in tongues in addition to the original citations. I highly recommend this book to anyone who desires to know more about the work of the Holy Spirit and the manifestations of the Spirit, especially the often misunderstood gift of tongues.

Vinson Synan, Ph.D.
Dean Emeritus
Regent University School of Divinity,
Virginia Beach, Virginia

Contents

Prologue — xi

Introduction — xv

Chapter 1 — 1
The Age of the Church Fathers and Mothers

Chapter 2 — 29
The Spiritual Significance of glossolalia-like prayer for the Fathers and Mothers of the Church

Chapter 3 — 37
Charisms in an Age of Upheaval

Chapter 4 — 45
A Time of Faith

Chapter 5 — 61
The Middle Ages

Chapter 6 — 87
Mystics—Singers of a New Song

Chapter 7 — 121
Into the Modern Era

Chapter 8 — 127
Jubilation and Tongues

Chapter 9 — 137
Toward the Future

Conclusion — 145

Contact the Author — 149

Parish Missions and Retreats — 149

Prologue

Lightening did not strike the evening I first experienced praying in tongues. I didn't see archangels. I simply found a comforting and quiet way of praying that calmed me and let me taste for a while the sweetness of God's presence.

Desperate and alone in a motel room in rural Texas before preaching at a Sunday service in a nearby Church, I found it impossible to pray.

There were many reasons I was desperate. I was studying at a Presbyterian seminary with high academic requirements. I suffered from yet undiagnosed right hemisphere brain dysfunction, probably from lack of oxygen at birth. This left me with many visual-spatial problems. I had illegible hand writing and limited ability to type with an old fashioned typewriter. I had attentional problems that kept me from staying focused in class. I felt crushed by the academic weight of an elephant.

In addition I struggled with the calling I had felt in my heart for years to become Catholic. The Presbyterian Church had been good to me. I loved much of Reformed theology, especially the writings of Karl Barth. I had served as summer student pastor and preached on weekends at Presbyterian churches that did not have a pastor. The struggle to decide to which faith community to give my life drained and left me paralyzed.

I was twenty-three and had never visited a prayer meeting or church where people prayed in tongues. Tongues were the last thing on my mind.

In that situation I did what most Protestant preachers would do when confronted with such major stress, I started to look through the Bible. My eyes fell on a passage in St. Paul that said when we do not know how to pray as we ought the Spirit prays through us in sighs too deep for words. That was what I needed, the Spirit praying through me.

Without thinking, I began to sigh. As the Scripture suggested, I invited the Spirit into my sighs. I gave control of my voice to God. Then the sighs changed into a comforting song without words. The sound nurtured me. A warm glow filled my heart. I lay there in peace for thirty minutes in the stillness, as waves of Divine love coursed through me.

When my praying in this strange "language" was finished, I rested in the stillness of God.

The next morning people were touched at my sermon in a way I had not seen congregations touched by my words before.

On the way back to my seminary I began to think of the experience. Was this what one of professors, also a leader in the charismatic renewal, called praying in tongues? I had earlier read an article by Killian McDonnel on the charismatic renewal in the Catholic Church and was theoretically aware of the gifts of the Spirit, especially tongues.

My charismatic professor, Rodman Williams (we called him Rod) held a prayer meeting in his home every Sunday night. I thought for a moment that I ought to go to that evening's prayer meeting. Maybe the people there could help me understand my experience.

Then reality crashed in. Entering the door of Dr. Williams' home would brand me at the seminary. I would be "one of those." And that brand could affect my future as a Presbyterian minister. Almost the entire faculty of the seminary ardently opposed Dr. Williams and they took noticed when a student started attending that prayer meeting. With everything else going on in my life I didn't feel like being branded.

I struggled hard, but ultimately decided to attend the prayer group that night.

About thirty-five people from all over the City of Austin attended that meeting as well as two or three students from the Presbyterian Seminary. About ten of the people came from St. Edward's University, the Catholic College in Austin. A beatific peace shined on most everyone's face.

A wondrous harmonious melody filled the room, like angels singing. I joined my voice with theirs. Later I was to learn that harmonious singing was jubilation which modern-day Pentecostals and charismatics called praying in tongues.

Afterward Rod and his wife Jo gave me a whole-hearted hug. As they prayed over me for a further release of the Spirit I felt showered by the very presence of God as the love of new brothers and sisters surrounded me.

Rod Williams knew I would want to understand more of this experience and he started me on an academic study and research plan that eventually led to this book.

Introduction

When she was a teenager, My Aunt Edna Earle's world changed. She found out that she had a new identity and family.

Edna Earle, my mother's youngest sibling was adopted out when she was two, following her mother's death of dengue fever. My mother, her oldest sibling, was sent to a Baptist orphanage in Troy Alabama, along with her brother Guthrie and her other sister Margaret.

Edna Earle grew up not knowing she had other family and thinking she was an only child, until, soon after they were adults, my mother, Uncle Guthrie and Aunt Margaret showed up on her doorstep

It startled her, scared her at first, but soon she entered into the joy and companionship of her family. They stayed close the rest of their years.

Most of us know stories of people finding out new information that gave them a more authentic identity.

Edna Earle discovered information about her origins that rocked her world. I think today, the Church is in a similar situation. As people keep turning to the original writing of the Church fathers, mothers and great spiritual leaders of the past, what they find could rock the Church.

For generations scholarship has done a good job of handing on the intellectual understanding of our heritage, but a poor one of presenting the human life behind those ideas.

Take for instance, Thomas Aquinas, arguably the best theologian of the last millennium. The original literature shows he prayed much like a modern Charismatic. It's possible to read many volumes by scholars on Aquinas and not know that he wept and sighed in his prayer and prayed aloud in the wordless speech we could call glossolalia. His great theological works such as his Summa Theologica were drenched in the tears of prayer. A scholar par excellence, he struggled in prayer, with tears, jubilation and sighs to allow the Spirit to guide him in his teaching and writing. Visions also played a vital role in how he went about doing the work of theology.

Where do you find such information, Deacon Ensley? Not usually in his modern biographies, but in the original sources, his own personal writings and his earliest biography by his contemporary and friend Bernard Gui.

Shocking as this may be, this is the picture the original sources paint. Perhaps scholars, when they did not include these passages in their writings, were embarrassed to do so. Perhaps, they considered them irrelevant.

Thankfully, some scholars, medievalists more than theologians, are taking that early information seriously and making it accessible to the rest of us.

You naturally may ask, Deacon Ensley, how do you know this about Aquinas? I would answer from Aquinas own words and from the words of those who knew him best.

He uses the word jubilation, which means a vocalized wordless prayer, essentially what modern Charismatics would call glossolalia, or praying in tongues. Listen to what he says:

First, (praying aloud) is a way in which we can stir ourselves with our words to pray with devotion. Secondly, praying aloud can keep our attention from wandering, because we can concentrate better if we support our feelings with words when we pray...when our mind is kindled by devotion as we pray, we break out spontaneously into weeping and sighing and cries of jubilation and other such noises...we have to serve the God to whom we offer reverence in prayer not only with our minds, but also with our bodies.[1]

We find lively worship and liturgy expanding throughout Christianity. Non-charismatic evangelicals now use many ways of expressive worship. In the Catholic Church, events presided over by our present Pope Francis and our two previous Popes could be quite lively. During World Youth Day celebrations in Rio de Janeiro, July 23-28, many worshippers in the crowds could be seen swaying from side to side, arms raised in the air, wearing rapt or joyous expressions on their faces.

Such scenes, along with on-stage appearances by celebrities such as Father Marcelo Rossi, a mega-church pastor whose records and movies regularly top the charts in his native Brazil, testified to the Catholic Charismatic Renewal's strong influence on the church in Latin America today.

Bernard Gui, his first biographer, describes Aquinas praying in this manner when he was at Mass, he "was utterly absorbed in the mystery, and his face ran with tears."

Thomas struggled in prayer while he was writing theology. Gui writes:

> He never set himself to study or argue a point, or lecture or write or dictate without first having recourse inwardly—but with tears—to prayer for the

---

[1] Simon Tugwell, ed. Albert and Thomas: Selected Writings (Classics of Western Spirituality) (New York: Paulist Press, 1988), 380.

understanding and the words required by the subject.[2]

Gui describes a scene when Thomas was teaching in Paris on Paul's writings and came to a difficult passage to interpret. He ordered his secretaries out of the room, "fell to the ground and prayed with tears,—then what he desired was given him and it all became clear."[3]

Such a catharsis, letting emotions out through jubilation, tears and fervent prayer and cries, attuned him to the spiritual world, and visions guided him at times in his groundbreaking teaching.

Reginald, his close aide and spiritual friend recalls hearing several voices coming out of Thomas' monastic cell, yet he knew that Thomas was alone. He persistently pressured Thomas to tell him what was going on until Thomas, "with tears running down his cheeks, said that his company had been the apostles Peter and Paul, whose holy presence had helped him resolve his questions about the passage in Isaiah."[4]

You may say isn't this an anomaly unique to Thomas.

Actually, it is only one of many hundreds of passages I found in my research. From the ending of the book of Acts until the seventeenth century, the literature of the Church abounds with stories such as Thomas Aquinas'. It includes major figures like St. Francis, Augustine, Ambrose, Teresa of Avila.

Nor is it limited to Holy people like Aquinas. Shocking new research shows whole congregations prayed this way

---

2   Bernard Gui *The Life of St. Thomas Aquinas*, ed. and trans. Kenelm Foster, O.P., contained in *The life of St. Thomas Aquinas: Biographical Documents* (Baltimore: Helicon Press, 1959), p.37.

3   Ibid., 38.

4   Ibid., 39.

for centuries.

The book of Acts did not end, it has continued through two thousand years of Church history. From the generation immediately after the Apostles until our own day, we have original writings telling a story that may be spiritually explosive; a story that can change our identity as Christians and give us a new family, as happened with my Aunt Edna Earle.

Not only will it help root us in our heritage, it can lead us into a wonderful and undreamed of future.

Step-by-step this book will guide you through those amazing writings and let you hear the voices of our ancestors in their own words.

The theme of this book may be seen by those who know me as out of character. I travel around the country 25 weeks a year teaching Contemplative prayer, deep quiet prayer in which our souls are knit together with God. I love a solemn, sedate Mass or Church service. God is present as well when jubilation and exuberant worship are not there. I like, in my personal prayer, the rich quiet whispers of the Spirit. But I also pray in jubilation, or as some would call it, in tongues.

Processing the insights from the tradition on expressive prayer and worship does not mean expressive prayer is the only way we pray. We can also pray in a contemplative manner, absorbed quietly in the Presence of God. Jubilation born out of the deep silences of prayer is richer and purer. Moreover, jubilation can dispose us to the stillness of contemplation.

There are seasons in our lives as individuals and as Church for both. It's not either/or but both/and.

CHAPTER 1

THE AGE OF THE CHURCH FATHERS AND MOTHERS

How sweet are the sighs and tears of prayer.
—St. Augustine of Hippo

Jubilation worketh wonder, 'Tis the harp the soul doth use.
—Meister Eckhard

Most of know how vital and alive the Christian faith was in the time of the Book of Acts. Acts depicts the Church as a warm family of believers who spread the faith of Jesus in an atmosphere of healing, tongues and miracles. Many people ask, what happened to this Church? Where did it go? Many people today think that it just disappeared. Actually it continued fervently for centuries.

How can you say that Deacon Ensley? Do you have a video? No, I don't have a video, but what we all have is the writings of Christians from the decades immediately after the time of the apostles until our own time that paint a picture of what Christian life was like. And in every generation from at least the fourth century on we find healings, miracles and the voicing of wordless expressions of faith.

We have writings in the church in every decade since the last book in the New Testament. However, writings are sparse during the first three centuries, the age of persecution by the Romans.

In 313, Constantine issued the Edict of Milan legalizing Christian worship. The persecution ended and soon Christianity became the religion of the Roman Empire.

Now, no longer being on the run like the Church before the time of Constantine, the Church had the time and resources to leave more detailed accounts of Christian life and worship.

Perhaps the greatest theologian and author of this period was Augustine of Hippo. Augustine had been a pagan but through the prayers of his mother became Christian.

Let's hear Augustine himself tell how Christ had led him so close to God:

> Late have I loved you, O Beauty ever ancient, ever new, late have I loved you! You called, you shouted, and you broke through my deafness. You flashed, you shone, and you dispelled my blindness...I have tasted you, now I hunger and thirst for more.[5]

Let's drop in on Easter Mass at the Church he pastored in the North African city of Hippo. It is part of a section of accounts from his famous book *The City of God*, which speaks of miracles most of which Augustine personally witnessed or heard about from his parishioners.

As Augustine tells the story personally, Easter Sunday dawned and crowds swarmed the Basilica of St. Stephen in Hippo, North Africa. Grasping onto the railing of the shrine, Paulus prayed fervently for a cure. Unexpectedly he fell prostrate, as Augustine put it, "as though in a trance." His usual convulsions stopped.

Augustine continues, "just as suddenly, he arose... The

---

5   Steven Fanning, *Mystics of the Christian Tradition* (London: Routledge, 2001), p. 78.

trembling had stopped."⁶

The crowd gazed on him with wonder.

According to Augustine, "The whole church soon rang with the clamor of rejoicing. Nearly everyone broke into loud prayers of thanksgiving."

People rushed up to where Augustine was sitting to tell him the whole story as the procession was about to begin.

Paulus, accompanied by a crowd stood in front of Augustine. Augustine raised him up to receive the kiss of peace.

Augustine describes the rejoicing crowd, "Cries of joy rose up everywhere: 'Thanks be to God.' No tongue was silent."

When the congregation finally stilled down, the Scriptures of Easter Day were read. Augustine cut his sermon short, saying, "I wanted to allow the people to meditate in their own minds on the divine eloquence of the divine deed rather than to listen to any mere words of mine."

Paulus stayed for dinner.

The third day of Easter, Augustine had the brother and sister stand in front of the congregation. Someone read an account of the miracle three days earlier as they stood before him. The contrast was clear, the young man stood there still without convulsing. His sister still convulsed. He dismissed the pair while many in the congregation prayed fervently that the sister also be cured.

Suddenly new joyful sounds emerged from people in the area of the shrine railing. Palladia had gone to the shrine immediately after Augustine dismissed them. She fell prostrate as though in a deep sleep then rose up cured.

---

6   Augustine, Gerald G. Walsh and Daniel J. Honan (translators) *The City of God*, Books XVII, XXII p. 448.

The congregation, seeing this, broke out in loud, spontaneous praise of God. Augustine himself describes the jubilation, "The exultation continued, and the wordless praise to God was shouted so loud that my ears could scarcely stand the din. But, of course, the main point was, in the hearts of this clamoring crowd, there burned that faith in Christ for which the martyr Stephen shed his blood.[7]

Augustine made clear that the healer in such miracles was the Resurrected Lord, "Now, the faith to which all these miracles bear witness is the faith that holds that Christ rose bodily from the dead and ascended with His flesh into heaven, because, of course, the martyrs were witnesses."[8]

This fervent prayer of the congregation happened not just when the Congregation gathered on Sunday but at times praise erupted when a small number of people gathered together.

Another moving account concerns a woman from Carthage who had been diagnosed with advanced breast cancer. No surgery could help. She prayed with her whole heart that God would heal her.

In a dream God, according to Augustine, instructed her to be at the Church at Hippo for the Easter baptisms and ask the first woman baptized to make the sign of the cross over her breast. She did that and was immediately healed as confirmed by her physician. For the most part she kept quiet about her encounter with the wondrous.

Augustine heard about her supposed healing and called her in reprimanding her for staying silent. He asked her to tell the story to her friends in his personal presence. Augustine wrote:

---

7   Ibid., 449.

8   Ibid., 450.

"I made her tell how the whole thing happened, from beginning to end, while the other women listened in great astonishment, and glorified God."[9]

Constantine's conversion to Christianity was a startling event of immeasurable importance for God's people.

The Church had grown in depth during the time of persecutions; it grew even more in the period of calm that began with the conversion of the emperor Constantine.

Great thinkers, great pastors and great saints gave strong theological and pastoral guidance to the Church. The Holy Spirit working through these shepherds and their flocks formed and shaped the early Christian tradition, and decided which books should be in the New Testament.

Issues such as the Trinity and the person of Christ were clarified. St. Augustine of Hippo, St. Ambrose of Milan, St. John Chrysostom, St. Gregory of Nyssa and many others were the charismatic shepherds of this period.

They, and other great thinkers and pastors of the Church during its first millennium, were known as the Fathers and Mothers of the Church.

From the fifth century until the eleventh, wave after wave of barbarian invasions disrupted the fabric of the Church. The period of calm ended.

The Church was not cowed by this. Beginning with Gregory the Great, in the late sixth century, the Church launched a massive missionary campaign that not only won back areas of Europe that had been lost to the faith, but extended the faith to new areas such as Germany, Poland and Scandinavia. Still, the constant disruption of barbarian invasions kept society and the Church in constant disruption.

---

9   Augustine of Hippo, *The City of God*, Digireads.com Publishing p. 612.

The Church converted the barbarians, but she was also influenced by them, and some of the quality of Church life was lost, to be restored in richer ways during the Age of Faith.

The last half of the first millennium of the Church was also marked by great thinkers. Among them were men of the stature of Pope Gregory the Great, Cassiodorus and Amalaris. The time from the conversion of Constantine until the dawning of the second millennium of the Church was the formative period of the Church—the era of the later Fathers, a time of lively faith but also a time of blood and storm.

This was the period in which the expressive worship tradition of the Church was shaped and formed and given the roots it needed to grow in richness in the following centuries.

A Time of Expressive Worship

The Church, after the Roman Empire became Christian, displayed a rich variety of styles of expressive prayer and worship. Congregations broke out in sounds of wonder, calling out phrases of praise and thanksgiving. The early writers depict them as sighing and weeping at times.

Jubilation during this formative period was a form of prayer without words, closely resembling the "tongues" of present-day charismatic renewal.

Jubilation referred to praying and singing aloud without words. Though consciousness of the role that this wordless prayer played in the tradition has grown very dim in the last hundred years, it played a very vital role in the formation of the liturgy until the ninth century in private prayer and in some group prayer until the late Middle Ages. Moreover, traces of it can be found in the mystical tradition as late as the nineteenth century.

ORIGIN OF THE WORD "JUBILATION"

The word "jubilation" or "jubilus" comes from the classical Latin word *Jubilatio* which means "loud shouting, whooping."[10]

In classical usage a jubilation was the pastoral call of a farmer or a shepherd.

It has been the age-old custom of country folk to call to one another or animals by using special calls or yodels.

One of the Church Fathers, St. Hilary (d. 368), knew of this use. In a discussion of jubilation among Christians, he refers to the peasant origins of the word: "And according to the custom of our language, we name the call of the peasant and agricultural worker a 'jubilus,' when in solitary places, either answering or calling, the jubilation of the voice is heard through the emphasis on the long drawn out and expressive rendering."[11]

This jubilation of the peasant was probably much like a yodel. In fact the word "yodel" comes from the medieval usage of the word jubilation.[12]

In the ancient world there were other forms of wordless expression besides the jubilus.

Sailors used a wordless cry called a *celusma*. In the city we find a form of wordless expression called *quiritare*.

(Wordless singing and wordless expression were quite

---

10 *Oxford Latin Dictionary* (Oxford: The Clarendon Press, 1973) Fascicle IV, p. 977.
11 St. Hilary, *Ennar. in Ps 65*, as found in George Chambers, *Folksong—Plainsong* (London: The Merlin Press, 1956), pp. 23-24.
12 *Die Musik In Geschichte unt Gegenwart* (Basel: Barenreiter Kassel, 1958), Vol. VII, p. 74.

common in pre-industrial societies.) We can still see examples of wordless songs and expression in modern society. Alpine shepherds still call to one another with long expressive yodels. Western ranch hands still herd cattle with a form of yodel.

Until the demise of the sailing ship, sailors would hoist canvas sails in unison with common calls such as "yo-heho."

The rhythms of nature and of life could flow through persons and be expressed in a variety of wordless expressions.

Farmers led agricultural animals such as sheep and goats by yodels and calls. Human muscle power in groups was still a vital source of energy. People working and lifting together regulated their work by group wordless calls. The Christians of the late Roman Empire and Dark Ages, were well acquainted with a variety of wordless expressions. When they prayed aloud wordlessly they saw this as the same type of activity that farmers and shepherds engaged in.

The Fathers and Mothers clearly saw wordless prayer and singing as a natural human activity and saw a strong identity between the spiritual jubilation of Christians and natural human jubilation.[13]

If they saw a great identity with their jubilation and the natural jubilation of the secular world, they also saw profound differences. For them, Christian jubilation was a natural human activity given over to a profoundly Christian and spiritual use.

Augustine could call Christian jubilation miraculous.[14]

---

13 A full discussion of the part that wordless yodels and cries played in classical society can be found in Chambers, *Folksong-Plainsong*, pp. 2-40.

14 "Our celusma, that we sing, is the miraculous Alleluia"—St. Augustine of Hippo (PL 40, p. 680).

Contrasting secular jubilation with Christian jubilation he wrote: "They jubilate out of confusion...we (the Christians) out of confession."[15] As we shall see later in the discussion of the spiritual significance of jubilation for the Fathers, and in the chapter on the relationship between tongues and jubilation, the Fathers saw jubilation as the continuation of a scriptural and apostolic tradition.[16] Certain scholars also found a continuation of the "tongues," the "spiritual song," and improvised worship of the New Testament and the apostolic era.

The Church Fathers and Mothers believed jubilation possessed profound spiritual and mystical significance. George Chambers in *Folksong—Plainsong* speaks about this change of use:

> Transferred to Catholic worship and prayer, it (jubilation) has at once an enhanced value; it is the expression of the soul in a higher sense; it ceases to be merely a subconscious utterance and becomes part of the spirit's yearning for the inner things of God.[17]

TYPES OF JUBILATION

Jubilation meant a variety of different things. As we look more closely at what the Fathers and Mothers say about it, we see three different main types of jubilation emerge.

In part because jubilation was not controversial, few early writers scrutinized it as closely as practices such as the controversy over pictures and statues received. Therefore the language about jubilation seems imprecise. The boundaries

---

15 St. Augustine of Hippo, (PL 40, p. 680).

16 "Our celusma, that we sing, is the miraculous Alleluia"—St. Augustine of Hippo (PL 40, p. 680).

17 Chambers, p. 5.

between the types are not clear, but three types can still be discerned.

The Fathers and Mothers held the view that jubilation was spontaneous outward expression of inner spiritual experience. It could be wordless songs or sounds but could also be manifested by bodily expressions such as gestures and laughter.

This experience of jubilation manifests itself generally in the following ways:

1. Musical jubilation is a form of spontaneous wordless singing. Modern music historians have studied this closely in the Church Fathers and Mothers.

2. Congregational jubilation is musical jubilation in a worship setting. Congregations sang an alleluia before the reading of the Gospel and extended the last "a" of the alleluia into a long spontaneous wordless song. Actually all singing in Church could be improvisational.

3. Mystical jubilation is closely related to musical jubilation. Early authors describe it as wordless sounds, often accompanied by laughter and gestures, during intense spiritual experience. Let's take a further look at these various forms of jubilation.

1. Musical Jubilation

Congregations expressed their yearning for God in wordless singing. Though it is unfortunate that theologians have not studied this aspect of patristic devotion, we are lucky to have the work of a number of medieval music historians on jubilation. These music historians have studied it intensely as they investigated the roots of Western music.

Albert Seay, a modern musical historian beautifully describes musical jubilation as, "an overpowering expression of the ecstasy of the spirit, a joy that could not be restricted to words...It occupied a peculiar place in the liturgy, for it carried implications of catharsis, a cleansing of the soul."[18]

Another musical source says that the jubilus was a sound "of joy and gratitude improvised upon the inspiration of the moment." Another major work dealing with the "jubilus" in detail, *Les Peres de L'Eglise* et *La Musique*, emphasizes its improvised nature: "One notes the more or less spontaneous impulse (of the jubilus). ...In (these jubilations) they exhaled joy to some extent without control."[19]

It is mentioned by many of the great Fathers and Mothers of the Church. Among them we find St. Augustine of Hippo, John Cassian, St. Ambrose of Milan, Peter Chrysologus, St. John Chrysostom, St. Gregory the Great, St. Isidore of Seville and Cassiodorus"—in short, most of the major thinkers of the Christian Church in the late Roman Empire and early Dark Ages.

(a) Augustine

St. Augustine of Hippo, after the New Testament, influenced the Church more than anyone else during the First Millennium. He mentions jubilation a number of times, especially in his *Commentary on Psalms*. He writes: "Where speech does not suffice...they break into singing on vowel sounds, that through this means the feeling of the soul may be expressed, words failing to explain the heart's conceptions. Therefore, if they jubilate from earthly exhilaration, should we not sing the jubilation out of heavenly joy, (singing) what words cannot express."

He urges his people to jubilate. He says: "You already

---

18 Albert Seay, *Music in the Medieval World* (Englewood Cliffs, New Jersey, 1965), p. 39.

19 Theodore Gerold, *Les Peres de l'Eglise el la Musique* (Paris: "Etudes d'Histoire et de Philosophic Religieuse"), p. 122.

know what it is to jubilate. Rejoice and speak. If you cannot express your joy, jubilate: jubilation expresses your joy, if you cannot speak; it cannot be a silent joy; if the heart is not silent to its God, it shall not be silent to his reward."[20]

Augustine noted the highly spontaneous and wordless character of jubilation:

> "He who sings a jubilus does not utter words; he pronounces a wordless sound of joy; the voice of his soul pours forth happiness as intensely as possible, expressing what he feels without reflecting on any particular meaning; to manifest his joy, the man does not use words that can be pronounced and understood, but he simply lets his joy burst forth without words; his voice then appears to express a happiness so intense that he cannot formulate it."[21]

Along the same line, he says: "What is jubilation? Joy that cannot be expressed in words; yet the voice expresses what is conceived within and cannot be explained verbally; this is jubilation."[22]

(b) Jerome

St. Jerome, the pioneer biblical scholar who translated the Bible into Latin, says of jubilation: "By the term *jubilus* we understand that which neither in words nor syllables nor letters nor speech is it possible to express or comprehend how much man ought to praise God."[23] In his translation of the book of Psalms he translated the Greek word *alalgma*, which means "shout of joy," as jubilus. When he uses the

---

20 Augustine, *Ennar. in Ps. 97*, 4—PL 37, pp. 1254-1255, translation Abbott David Geraets O.S.B.
21 Augustine, *Ennar. in Ps. 99*, 4—PL 37, p. 1272, Geraets.
22 Augustine *Ennar. in Ps. 94*, 4—PL 37, p. 1272, Geraets.
23 PL 26. 970.

word *jubilus* in this regard, he more than likely has in mind the experience of wordless singing that was common in his day and expressed in his definition of jubilation.

For hundreds of years after, when people read the words *jubilatio, jubilare* and *jubilus* in the Latin Bible, the Vulgate, it called to mind their own experience of wordless song and prayer.

(c) St. John Chrysostom

The best known Father of this time in the East, St. John Chrysostom, the bishop of Constantinople, encouraged his people to sing without words. He says: "It is permitted to sing psalms without words, so long as the mind resounds within. For we do not sing for men, but for God who can hear even our hearts and penetrate into the secrets of our soul."[24]

(d) Cassiodorus (490-583)

Cassiodorus lived in the time when the old Roman civilization had neared complete collapse and the countryside was in disruption because of various barbarian tribes. A monk, deeply devoted to prayer, he was also a man who intensely believed in education at a time when the light of learning was growing dim.

In the midst of wars he did several things to preserve learning. Perhaps the most important was to write syllabi to guide students in both sacred and secular education. An essential part of education was to know Scripture and the Latin and Greek commentators on Scripture. The first book for "soldiers of Christ" to read in the Scriptures was the book of Psalms. To help them with this study of the psalms he wrote a massive commentary in which he comments on

---

24 Alfred Sendry, *Music in Ancient Israel* (New York: Philosophical Library, 1969) p. 201.

jubilation eight or ten times.

For him jubilation was an overwhelming joy. He says: "The jubilation is called an exultation of the heart, which, because it is such an infinite joy, cannot be explained in words." Again, "Jubilation is said to be an excessive joy, but not the sort that can be explained in words."[25]

Jubilation, for him, could be a loud and fervent shout. He says: "Now, jubilation is the joy expressed with fervor of mind and shout of indistinct voice."

It is a response to Jesus the incarnation who, as Psalm 32:3 says, is the "new song." All the universe has been filled "with saving exultation" because of that event.[26]

It is a "helping," a "delighting," "for those for whom the exultation of words was not able to be sufficient, so they might leap forth into the most overflowing and unexplainable joy... At the same time it teaches the believer to give thanks. Part of the purpose of jubilation is "teaching rejoicing souls that they ought to give thanks to the Lord, not to sing confused by some anxiety."[27]

Jubilation is an overwhelming joy for him that bursts out from the heart into the voice. He says: "Jubilation...with great delight leaps with joy into the voice. What the speech of a confused voice cannot explain, the devout bursting forth of the rejoicing believer declares."[28]

Cassiodorus' words tremble with wonder at jubilation. For him it is both an astounding joy that bursts forth by means of the voice and a teacher that teaches the Christian how to give thanks in the right way.

---

25 M. Aureli Cassiodori, *Exposition in Psalterium Ps.65*, 1, in PL 70, p. 451.

26 M. Aureli Cassiodori, *Ps. 32*, 3 in PL 70, p. 226.

27 M. Aureli Cassiodori, *Ps. 80*, 1 in PL 70, p. 586.

28 M. Aureli Cassiodori, *Ps. 97*, 5 in PL 70, pp. 689-690.

(e) St. Isidore of Seville

St. Isidore (d. 636), the bishop of Seville, became one of the most venerated scholars of the Middle Ages. He passed on much of the wisdom of the Latin Fathers to later generations. He mentions jubilation several times. For him it was a breathtaking experience. He says: "Language cannot explain…words cannot explain. …It is an effusion of the soul… When the joy of exultation erupts by means of the voice, this is known as jubilation."[29]

A Widespread Form of Private Prayer

Jubilation could be an ordinary form of prayer for believers in the Christian Roman Empire. When they sang wordlessly they extended vowel sounds like that after the singing of an alleluia. Sometimes, they sang the jubilation without the alleluia. It was a widespread form of individual prayer. Jerome mentions farmers in the field and even little children praying in this way. Others mention Christian sailors and boatmen on the Loire praying the jubilation. It was so widespread that Marie Pieriki, an historian of medieval music, has said: "This ejaculation (song-prayer), modulated on all forms, became the refrain of gladness which accompanied the daily occupations of the peaceful population converted to the new faith."[30]

2. Congregational Jubilation

Jubilation played a significant role in group worship and prayer for hundreds of years, becoming a standard part of the Mass.

Improvised Music. This form of improvised song-prayer

---

29   St. Isidore of Seville, *Opera Omnia* V, 43.

30   Marie Pieriki, *Song of the Church.*

developed when the churches had a considerable degree of spontaneity in their worship. Besides jubilation, the music of psalms and hymns could be improvised. Also, as we shall see later in more detail, congregations could react spontaneously with laughter, tears, and sighs and by shouting phrases such as "Glory to God."

It appears that most of the music in the patristic era, and at least some of it until the time of Amalaris in the ninth century, had an improvised nature: *L'encyclopedic de la Musique* says:

> From these sources (i.e., the Church Fathers) one senses clearly that the music of the Christian era was originally improvised. The first Christians expressed their religious ecstasy in a purely emotional and spontaneous fashion by means of music. According to the terminology of Tertullian, all the members of an assembly were invited to participate in the praise of God by words from Scripture or by "songs of their own invention." The first Christian authors, Hilary Poitiers (315-366) and Jerome (340-420) and Augustine (354-430), until Amalaris (ninth century), describe the rich, exuberant coloraturas sung without a text and the alleluia songs as overwhelming melody of joy and gratitude sung upon the inspiration of the moment. A large number of the melodies that have come down to us still have traces of improvisation.[31]

Still, the Church Fathers and Mothers warned against excessive enthusiasm in music, especially if it resembled the music of the theater or the streets. The debate among them on whether to use instruments and hymns in church indicates their desire to set limits on exuberance. Still they praised the emotion and improvised nature of music.

---

31 *L'encyclopedic de la Musique*, article "improvisation."

St. John Chrysostom suggests that it is the work of the Holy Spirit that makes improvised singing in churches possible. He says: "Though men and women, young and old, are different, when they sing hymns, their voices are influenced by the Holy Spirit in such a way that the melody sounds as if sung by one voice."[32]

For him, improvised singing helped unite people. Chrysostom felt so excited about singing that he calls the cantor the "prophet" and music "prophecy."

An interesting passage gives a glimpse of the way singing took place at the Church of Holy Peace in Constantinople. Chrysostom says: "The prophet speaks and we all respond to him. All of us make echo to him. Together we form one choir. In this, earth imitates heaven. This is the nobility of the Church."[33]

The Fathers and Mothers also describe congregational singing as a joining in with the voices of angels.

Says Basil: "What, then is more blessed than to imitate on earth the choirs of angels."[34] And Chrysostom declared: "For when we sing, the angels blend their voices with ours and we blend our voices with theirs; for the angels of heaven don't have anything else to do but sing the praises of God eternally."[35]

This congregational singing could deeply move people. Augustine tells of how he was stirred in the early days of his conversion when he heard church singing: "How abundantly did I weep to hear those hymns of thine, being touched to hear those hymns of thine, being touched to the

---

[32] As quoted in Alfred Sendrey, *Music in Ancient Israel*, p. 198.
[33] Chrysostom, as quoted in *L'encyclopedic des musiques sacres*, Vol. 2, p. 15.
[34] St. Basil, Letters, trans. *Agnes Clare Way* (Catholic University Press, 2010) p. 7.
[35] Chrysostom, *In Psalmos* 8, 1.

very core by thy sweet Church songs."³⁶

The jubilation came after the singing of the alleluia, just before the Gospel during Mass. During the celebration of Mass, as the congregation and choir sang the last alleluia, the people moved into exuberant wordless singing on vowel sounds. This jubilation could last up to five minutes. In a real sense it was a preparation for the hearing of the Gospel. This improvised jubilation blended their hearts as they expressed joy and exuberance.

Cassiodorus gives us a vivid description of congregational worship in his time. "The tongue of singers rejoices in it; joyfully the community repeats it. It is an ornament of the tongue of singers...like something good of which one can never have enough. It is innovated in ever-varying jubilations."³⁷

During the ninth century, improvisation ceased to be an expected part of the liturgy. One of the reasons for this is the cumulative effect of taking in whole nations into the Christian Church.

From the period of Pope St. Gregory, in the sixth century until the eleventh century, the Church was taking in new nations and barbarian tribes. Tribes and nations were often converted en masse. While these were real conversions, it often took generations for a vital Christianity to filter down to the ordinary people. This made improvisation, which relied to some extent on spiritual sensitivity on the part of congregations, a difficult thing. Until the tenth or eleventh century the waves of barbarian disrupted Europe, keeping it under siege. These two factors caused Church music to be done more and more by trained choirs and resulted in Church music being written in musical notation,

---

36   As quoted in Paul Henry Lang, *Music in Western Civilazation*, 1941) p. 48.

37   As quoted in Chambers, p. 7.

thus losing much of its improvised character.

The jubilation was to a large extent replaced by the musical sequence. In the year 860 Norsemen sacked the cloister of Jumieges in Normandy and a monk carried with him the written musical notation for the Mass to the safety of the monastery at St. Gall. There a young monk named Notker, reading over its contents, noticed that words had been written in place of the jubilations after the final of the alleluia. Notker took the hint and composed other words to replace jubilations.

At first this was a memory device to help remember melodies, but soon it replaced the jubilation.[38] Though jubilation ceased to be an expected part of the liturgy, one can still find large groups of ordinary people improvising expressive jubilations well into the Middle Ages, and mystically oriented small groups entering into heartfelt jubilations at least into the seventeenth century.

3. Mystical Jubilation

Mystics are people who feel in a special way the tug of eternity. Their lives are marked by a hunger for God. Their search for intimacy with God carries them through a radical transformation, often marked by dark tunnels and moments of indescribable ecstasy. This intimacy with God helped them love their brothers and sisters in Christ more and more with the same love they experienced from God.

Many felt the pull of God during this time. Among the heroes of this age were the ascetics of the desert who gave themselves over to constant prayer and radical transformation. *The Life of Anthony* by Athanasius, *The Life of Paul the Hermit* by Jerome, *The Sayings of the Fathers* and many other similar writings pictured radical ascetics living

---

38 Henry Osborn Taylor, *The Medieval Mind* (London: Macmillan and Co. Ltd., 1911), vol. 2, p. 201.

in deserted places giving themselves over to constant prayer and a radical following of the Gospel. They would often emerge from long years of prayer as men of great tenderness whose very presence brought healing to disturbed souls. Many others who were more moderate in their asceticism also followed the call to prayer. The monastery at Nola headed by St. Paulinus and his wife St. Therasia (late fourth and early fifth century) is an example of this style.

Part of the prayer experience of those who gave themselves over to transforming prayer involved outward physical expression of the deep inward moving of the Spirit. This was at times expressed in jubilation. Jubilation when it was part of transforming prayer was often quite a bit more spontaneous and fervent than the more ordinary jubilation of the liturgy. Traces of mystical jubilation can be seen in the patristic era. Later in the medieval period mystical jubilation becomes much more common.

Pope Gregory the Great, who is quoted a number of times on jubilation in the Middle Ages, appears to be talking about this in some passages in his commentary on Job. He describes it as an immense interior joy that is manifested outwardly by the voice, physical gestures and laughter. He says: "What we mean by the term jubilation is when we conceive such a great joy in the heart that we cannot express it in words; yet despite this the heart vents what it is feeling by means of the voice what it cannot express by discursive speech."[39]

Jubilation could also be expressed in bodily gestures, according to Gregory. Jubilation with gestures became a common experience among men of prayer in later periods. Gregory says: "What we call jubilation is an unspeakable joy which can neither be concealed nor expressed in words. It betrays itself, however, by certain gestures, though it is

---

39 St. Gregory the Great, *Mor. in Job*, 8, 88.

not expressed in any suitable words."[40] One of the points Gregory makes, and is quoted on through the centuries, is that jubilation is a joy that cannot be concealed and cannot be expressed in words. He says: "By the term jubilation we mean a joy of the heart that cannot be expressed in speech, yet the person who is rejoicing makes this joy known in certain ways—this joy that cannot be concealed, yet cannot be fully expressed (in words)."[41]

This jubilation for him is, in part, a struggle—a struggle to fully express praise and joy. Angels can praise perfectly, but men who suffer the limitations of speech cannot express this praise and joy in speech and therefore must jubilate. He says: "Let angels therefore praise because they know such brightness; but let men, who are limited by speech, jubilate."[42]

Gregory pictures heaven as a place of laughter and jubilation:

> The mouth is rightly said to be filled with laughter, the lips with jubilation, since in that eternal land, when the mind of the righteous is borne away in transport, the tongue is lifted up in praise.

For Gregory, jubilation is the spontaneous outward response to inward spiritual experience. It expresses itself in wordless sounds by means of the voice, by gestures and by laughter. There is a struggle involved in jubilation—the struggle of not being able to praise God in the perfect way that angels praise him. When words fail, men must jubilate. Jubilation and laughter are the praise of the blessed in heaven.

We find this more mystically-oriented form of jubilation

---

[40] Gregory the Creat, *Morals on the book of Job*, translated by J. Bliss (Google books) vol 3 p. 56.

[41] Gregory, *Mor. in Job*, 28, 35.

[42] Gregory, *Mor. in Job*, 28, 35.

in the writings of John Cassian, who lived in the early fifth century and helped to interpret the experience of the desert holy men and women for Western Europe. His writings exerted an influence for centuries on Western spirituality. He speaks of monks waking with "a sacrifice of jubilations." It played a part in his understanding of mystical experience. Ecstasy is a commonly mentioned experience among men and women of deep prayer. It is the experience of being carried beyond oneself when one is caught up in the presence of God. An experience of jubilation could accompany this sort of ecstasy. Sometimes the delight of this experience is so great that the monk breaks out into shouts. Cassian describes this experience: "For often through some inexpressible delight and keenness of spirit the fruit of a most salutary conviction arises so that it actually breaks forth into shouts owing to the greatness of its uncontrollable joy; and the delight of the heart and the greatness of exultation make themselves heard even in the cell of the neighbor." Sometimes this experience of God is felt in profound quiet; sometimes it is expressed by "a flood of tears." Prayer without words, be it shouts, quiet or tears, has great value: "That is not a perfect prayer...wherein the monk understands himself and the words which he prayed."[43]

OTHER STYLES OF EXPRESSIVE PRAYER AND WORSHIP

The picture that emerges from reading the literature of the early Church is that people could be quite expressive both in private and public worship. St. Augustine of Hippo, who was the pastor and bishop of the Christian Church in Hippo during the early fifth century, has left us many

---

43 John Cassian, "Praying in a Transport of Mind." This is an unidentified quote found in *The Soul Afire* (Garden City, New York: Image Books, A Division of Doubleday and Co., 1973), pp. 362-363.

interesting accounts of the spontaneity of his congregation. One Augustinian scholar, Frederick Van Der Meer, has said of their Church behavior: "Augustine's congregation was in the habit of reacting to whatever was read or preached with all the liveliness of their temperament. They shouted comments, sighed, and laughed, like children at a cinema."[44] This spontaneity can be seen in Augustine's description of psalm-singing. Augustine describes what might be a typical spontaneous reaction during psalm-singing: "You will see him singing with intense emotion, with the expression of his face adapting itself to the spirit of the psalm and with tears often coursing down his cheeks. He sighs between the words that he sings, and whoever has no special skill in reading men's thoughts will be wholly taken in by the outward appearance and will say: 'How deeply this lad is stirred as he listens to this psalm!' See how he sighs, how deeply he sighs.—And then the man in his turn begins again to sing and puts into the song all the power that is in him. Yes, he sings with the very marrow of his bones, with voice, face and profound sighs all showing how deeply he is stirred."[45]

We also have some impressive accounts of expressive worship from *Egeria—The Diary of a Pilgrimage*. This is the account of a woman from Gaul who made a pilgrimage to Christian Palestine in the early fifth century. She commented on all she saw and left us some vivid accounts of worship in the Christian churches of Jerusalem during this period. Her work is a major source for liturgists. The people of Jerusalem were quite devout and she says that the houses of the city were emptied on Sundays because people flocked to church. They loved ceremony and candlelight processions. One of their customs was to gather in the church on Sundays well before daybreak to hear a special

---

44 F. Van Der Meer, *Augustine the Bishop* (New York: Sheed and Ward, 1961), p. 339.
45 Van Der Meer, p. 336.

reading of the account of Jesus' resurrection. This was known as the *resurrectio Domini*. Thus every Sunday for them was an Easter. When the reader would read the account of the death and resurrection of the Lord the people would be deeply moved. The account says: "As soon as the reading of it (the account of the resurrection) has begun, so much moaning and groaning is heard that the hardest of men would be moved to tears because the Lord has endured so much on our behalf."[46] Holy Week and Easter could be special times of ceremony in the City of Jerusalem, the city where the very events commemorated had taken place. Crowds of thousands, with lighted candles, would retrace the Lord's footsteps during Holy Week. During the outdoor ceremony marking the arrest of the Lord, people outside the city could be so moved that the sound of their emotions could be heard in the city. Egeria says: "During the reading of the passage (about the arrest of the Lord) there is such moaning and groaning with weeping from all the people that their moaning can be heard practically as far as the city."[47]

These and other passages from Egeria's *Diary of a Pilgrimage* point to another aspect of expressive, wordless worship— the aspect of being moved to sorrow and deep religious emotion. The passages quoted on jubilation primarily speak of a wordless form of prayer that indicated an overwhelming joy. Here we have a wordless form of prayer that indicates a different sort of experience. It is the experience of being deeply touched, but not necessarily abundantly joyful. It indicates a different moment in Christian experience.

These "moans, groans, and weepings" recall Romans 8:26 where Paul speaks of the Holy Spirit praying through

---

[46] *Egeria The Diary of a Pilgrimage*, trans. George E. Gingres (Paramus, N.J., Newman Press, 1970), p. 92.

[47] *Egeria*, p. 109.

believers with sighs too deep for words.

Ordinarily the words "moan," "groan" and "sigh" suggest a response to a bad experience. These and similar words are used in this period and in the Middle Ages to describe a response to religious experience. What is being described is not a gruesome experience such as words like "groan" and "moan" suggest, but a voiced wordless response to a particular religious event. The sounds likely express the type of religious experience the person is going through. So rather than suggest something gruesome, the words "moan" and "groan" are probably indications of the wordless religious sounds the people expressed in their worship without the connotations that such words normally have. In fact one wonders if the phrase "wordless sounds" ought not to be substituted for "moan" and "groan."

One of the important things about the account of the worship of the Church in Jerusalem is the way expressive prayer was tied to liturgical prayer. The response of the people came from hearing of the Word in a liturgical celebration. The people were so attuned to the liturgy, so moved by it, so open to expressing their devotion in spontaneous ways that they naturally expressed their feelings in wordless sounds and tears. The type of experience described by Egeria appears to be a kindred type of response to jubilation. Egeria describes the more reflective moment, the moment of pathos, the moment of contrition. Both the "moans" and "groans" of Egeria and the joyful wordless sounds of jubilation are in a real sense glossolalia prayer—wordless, spontaneous prayer that is spoken aloud.

Sighs, tears, wordless sounds and body gestures could all play a part in personal prayer. In the fourth and fifth centuries people prayed much more than they do today. There are descriptions of farmers praying in the fields and women praying while spinning. Ambrose suggests that the whole evening for Christians be spent in hymns, psalm-singing and prayer, and the indications are that many people followed his suggestion.

Augustine describes the people in his church praying in expressive ways. Van Der Meer summarizes Augustine on this point: "Men uttered their prayers out loud and much more often than they do today; they prayed straight from the heart and accompanied their prayer with lively gestures... Many prayed with sighs and tears... A man did not feel any sense of embarrassment when he stepped before the altar in torn clothes and with disheveled hair, and broke into loud sobs about his troubles."[48]

"How sweet," Augustine said in his commentary on the Psalms, "are the sighs and tears of prayer."[49] Common gestures were outstretched hands, prostrations, kneeling, loud beating of the breast, and the throwing of oneself on the floor in contrition.

Augustine encouraged his people to pray with outstretched hands. Augustine felt that such gestures could be of spiritual benefit if they were done with a right attitude. He gave the following advice to a widow who was praying about the death of her son: "The bending of the knee, the stretching out of hands, and the sighs may well come from a genuine motion of the Spirit and so serve to make prayer more sincere."[50]

Augustine also knew that expressive prayer was not the central element in prayer. The important thing for him was the attitude of heart on the part of the believer. A man could go through fervent bodily gestures and his prayer could be insincere. He said to his congregation once: "You throw

---

48   Van Der Meer, p. 169.

49   St. Augustine of Hippo, *Enar in Ps.* 125.

50   Van Der Meer, p. 169.

your bodies to the ground, you bend your necks... I see where your body lies but I ask myself where your spirit is; I see your limbs stretched out, but show me whether your attention is standing upright or whether it has not been washed away by the flood of your thoughts."[51]

---

51 Van Der Meer, p. 169.

CHAPTER 2

THE SPIRITUAL SIGNIFICANCE OF GLOSSOLALIA-LIKE PRAYER FOR THE FATHERS AND MOTHERS OF THE CHURCH

The Jubilus urges the flock to climb lofty mountains.
—St. Peter Chrysologus

In our own day we have witnessed a rebirth of voiced, wordless prayer, most often referred to as "speaking in tongues." A more technical term for "speaking in tongues" is glossolalia. Pentecostals and charismatics consider it a gift of prayer. Under the inspiration of the Spirit, the person prays or sings aloud without words, expressing things which cannot be spoken in words. The importance for charismatics is not that it is a language or "unknown tongue," but that it is a means of the Holy Spirit praying through the believer expressing in sounds things that are beyond conceptual language. A leading theologian, George Montague, sees glossolalia not as a language but as pre-conceptual prayer.[52]

As we shall see in the chapter that deals with the relationship between "tongues" and jubilation, most biblical scholars

---

52   Montague discusses this viewpoint in detail in *The Spirit and His Gifts* (New York: Paulist Press, 1974), pp. 18-29.

consider New Testament "tongues" as "ecstatic speech," wordless sounds rather than actual spoken language. Also, modern society has recently been rediscovering what pre-industrial societies seem to know instinctively, namely that communication and expression are much broader than the vocabulary and syntax of a particular language. The use of phrases such as "body language," "good vibes" and "bad vibes" indicates rediscovery of this. So certain types of glossolalia can be real language communication in the broader sense of the term even if that language does not correspond to a language with syntax and vocabulary. Since the important understanding of glossolalia is not that it is a "foreign language," but that it is preconceptual prayer, jubilation as the Fathers describe it certainly qualifies as glossolalia. In fact, the definition given to glossolalia in a major study of the subject by Morton Kelsey sounds much like the definitions of jubilation given by the Church Fathers. Kelsey says: "It (glossolalia) is a spontaneous utterance of uncomprehended and seemingly random speech sounds."[53]

It must also be added that the many references in patristic and later literature to "sighs" and "groans" should also be understood as a glossolalia-like prayer. The spontaneous repetition of sounds as prayer closely resembles the description of prayer given by Paul: "The Spirit helps us when we do not know how to pray, praying through the believer with 'sighs too deep for words' " (Rom. 8:26).

This passage, often used by charismatics to describe the Holy Spirit as praying through the believer in tongues, is considered by some Scripture scholars as a probable "glossolalia" reference. One major difference in the Fathers' understanding of glossolalia prevalent in Pentecostal and neo-Pentecostal circles is that the Fathers saw it as a

---

53 Morton T. Kelsey, *Tongue Speaking* (Garden City, New York: Doubleday, 1968), p. 1.

natural human activity. The word that they used to describe glossolalia, jubilation, could also describe the secular yodel of agricultural workers or war cries. The Fathers knew this. There is a tendency in some Pentecostal circles to see glossolalia as somehow apart from normal human experience. Analogies are almost never drawn with similar human activities such as yodeling, humming in the shower, etc. In fact, one wonders if the reaction of misunderstanding and occasional fear that some Christians outside Pentecostal circles have of glossolalia does not come from this setting apart of glossolalia from normal human activities.

If the Fathers could see jubilation as a natural human activity they could also see it as a form of prayer that had profound spiritual significance. It was a natural human activity given over to Christian use. An analogy can be made with the Eucharist. Sitting down to a meal is one of the most ordinary human activities. The Eucharist is also a meal; it is also ordinary and human. The difference in the Eucharist and a family meal is that the Eucharist is a meal given over to a real and profound encounter with the total Christ.

The Eucharist is still ordinary, and much of the richness of our understanding of it comes from the use of ordinary elements, but it is also profoundly spiritual. The same can be said of the Fathers' understanding of glossolalia as an ordinary human activity, the activity of giving over one's voice to a flow of sounds from the subconscious. They saw it as the same type of experience as battle cries, yodels, and humming. Yet among Christians this ordinary activity was given over to the deep movement of the Spirit within the person—a physical, vocal giving of oneself to the move of the Spirit.

A part of the spiritual significance for the Fathers was that jubilation was a means of God praying in the Christian.

Augustine clearly puts this view forward in his commentary on Psalm 32. In his commentary he says that men do not know how to pray or sing to God in the right way. God himself helps through jubilation. In jubilation, God himself helps form the tune. Augustine says: "Lo and behold, he sets the tune for you himself, so to say; do not look for words, as if you could put into words the things that please God. Sing in jubilation: singing well to God means, in fact, just this: *singing in jubilation*."[54]

In what appears to be a paraphrase of Paul's statement in Romans 8:26 that the Spirit prays through us with struggle and we do not know how to pray as we ought, Augustine continues: "The jubilus is a melody which conveys that the heart is in travail over something it cannot bring forth in words. (When you cannot say what you want to say) what else can you do but jubilate?"[55]

So we also see that for Augustine jubilation was a real catharsis, a means of God praying through the believer. This same sentiment is expressed with the use of beautiful, imaginative imagery by St. Peter Chrysologus. For him, jubilation was a means of God refreshing, leading and challenging the believer. He saw jubilation as God's own song. He expresses this in imagery that calls to mind the original meaning of the word jubilation, the call of a shepherd. He pictures Jesus as the shepherd that calls the sheep by means of the shepherd's yodel, the jubilation.

Chrysologus' description of jubilation in his commentary on Psalm 94 (95 in Hebrew Bible) breaks into poetry as he describes the call of the shepherd:

> The Shepherd with sweet jubilus, with varied

---

54 St. Augustine of Hippo, *On the Psalms* (Westminster, Maryland: The Newman Press, 1961), vol. 2, pp. 111-112.

55 Augustine, *On the Psalms*, pp. 111-112.

melody, leads the flock to pasture, keeps the tired flock at rest under shaded grove. This jubilus urges the flock to climb lofty mountains, there to graze on healthful grasses.

Also it calls them to descend to the low valleys slowly and without hurry. How happy are those sheep that join their voices to the voice of the Shepherd, that follow when he calls to feed and gather. They truly jubilate to their Shepherd... In (singing) psalms let us jubilate.[56]

So great was the spiritual and mystical significance of jubilation to the Fathers that they even considered it miraculous. Augustine could say: "Our celusma (wordless call) which we sing is the miraculous Alleluia."[57]

The *Life of St. Germanus* gives an account of a miracle worked through jubilation. The soldiers of an army fighting in Roman Britain against pagan tribes feared that they would lose a battle against overwhelming odds.

Just before the battle they were baptized into the Christian Church. Wet with baptismal waters they placed their confidence in God rather than in arms. Many dropped their armaments. The pagans saw this and gloated over what they thought would be an easy victory.

St. Germanus told the soldiers that he would give them a war-call that would defeat the enemy, the jubilation. The soldiers sang the alleluia three times and then joined as one man on the jubilation. According to the account the pagans dropped their arms and fled across the river.[58]

---

56   St. Peter Chrysologus, *Sermo VI in Ps 99*. 6. P.L. 40, p. 680.
57   P.L. 40, p. 680.
58   *The Western Fathers*, translated by F. R. Hoare (New York: Sheed and Ward, 1954), p. 301.

Regardless of the accuracy of the story, it shows the high regard in which the Christians of those times held the jubilation.

Christians of this period viewed jubilation as an entering into the music of angels or of heaven. "Heaven," said St. Isidore, "functions under the rhythm of jubilation." [59] This was also suggested by St. Gregory the Great in his discussion on jubilation when he described jubilation as the praise of the blessed in heaven.

Though the idea of praying and singing aloud without words seems strange to us, it was not to the Fathers. They were aware, much more than we today, that a person is his or her body. To pray, at least in part, we have to use our voices and our limbs in prayer. The Fathers and Mothers saw God as a wondrous mystery and much of what God wanted to do in Christians was a wondrous mystery. So praying and singing without words could be a way of entering into that mystery, that part of God that is too great for ordinary words. It was a means of penetrating into that mystery, of being led into that mystery with both body and soul.

Jubilation was a confession of faith. Augustine called it confession, Cassiodorus a "declaration." It was a witness that much of God was beyond us, a witness that he prayed through his people and united their voices. Even today, the traces of jubilation that remain in Gregorian chant and in plain song eloquently describe that mystery.

As we have seen jubilation and improvised singing unite men and women of divergent backgrounds within a congregation. The blending of their voices led to a blending of hearts. Though jubilation was often spoken of as a spontaneous expression of joy, it could also be something one entered regardless of feelings. Augustine, Chrysologus and others

---

[59] As found in Chambers, p. 8.

used the imperative form of the verb jubilate. In short, they commanded people to jubilate. Jubilation, improvised jubilation, was a regular part of the liturgical life of the people. It was something that they entered into in season and out of season, in times of aridity and of consolation. In a sense, jubilation, for them, was an opening up of a channel for God to work and pray through them. It was an entering into the praise of heaven.

The Fathers and Mothers of the Church believed it was natural to pray with both voice and body. They knew that much of God and much of our encounter with God were wondrous mystery. It was also natural that they should express this, and in part experience it, by means of sound and song without words. For them there was a song, a rhythm in the heart of God; their jubilation opened them that mystery to them.

CHAPTER 3

CHARISMS IN AN AGE OF UPHEAVAL

Stories, at times firsthand, of healings and miracles, abounded in the Age of the Fathers and Mothers as we have already seen in our glimpse of Augustine's parish in Hippo. Accounts of miracles during these early periods are so many that it would take a book much longer than this to include them all. Still we can pause from our discussion of glossolalia and peek at accounts of the wondrous to give us a context for the study of glossolalia. When jubilation and expressive worship flourished, so did the wondrous.

Let's pause for a moment in our discussion of glossolalia prayer to look at a snapshot of Church life in an early period called the Dark Ages, beginning after the Fall of Rome.

In the late sixth century, warring barbarian tribes fought with the armies of the eastern empire for the control of Rome. For over a hundred years before that, Rome and all Italy had been in the grip of warfare and upheaval. The city of Rome itself, which passed from one side to the other several times, was only a shadow of its former glory; the city that once numbered over a million inhabitants now numbered less than 40,000. One inhabitant at the time said, "We see before our eyes this very city, the walls shaken by storms, houses ruined, churches overthrown, and buildings rotten with old age collapsing." Vast areas of the Roman Empire—such as Britain and Gaul—that had once been Christian, were now in the hands of pagan tribes.

The Dark Ages

This was the beginning of the period many historians call the dark ages. While it may be considered dark, in the sense that the social and political structures of a mighty empire collapsed, it can hardly be considered a dark period for the Christian faith. In the midst of this disorder we have many examples of the Lord moving powerfully among his people, leading them to missionary activity, helping them form strong, loving Christian communities, and encouraging and guiding them with signs and wonders.

During this era, missionaries began to walk boldly into areas which had been taken over by pagan tribes and brought them back to the Lord. They converted tens of thousands to Christ in North Germany, Scandinavia and Poland where the Gospel had never been preached before. This is the Rome of Pope Gregory the Great, and it is also the era of some remarkable charismatic activity which he recorded. Gregory himself had not wanted to be Pope. Most of all he wanted to be a man of continual prayer; he wanted to follow, as he called it, "the way of the angels." But because of his popularity and reputed holiness, the people and the clergy of Rome elected him Pope. One early tradition says that he had to be dragged from the monastic community where he was abbot to be consecrated bishop.

He was evidently not a weak man or easily cowed by the circumstances of his day. In the midst of social and political upheavals, he planned and launched missionary ventures that reconverted the northern parts of the Empire. At home he built Christian guesthouses where victims of the famine and warfare in the countryside could come for refuge.

His writings tell us a lot about how the charismatic gifts operated during that era. In one of his major works, the Dialogues, and in his sermons, we can find scores of accounts of prophecies, healings and visions that people were experiencing in his own day and as early as 70 years before that. Gregory believed that healings, miracles and the prophetic gifts were important to the Church, and that they should be integrated into the whole context of the Christian life.

SCORES OF HEALINGS AND VISIONS

One of the accounts tells of a mother whose little boy had died. She was walking down the road carrying him in her arms when she met Libertinus, a monk, who was noted for his deep prayer life. She implored him, "You shall not pass until you have brought my son back to life!"[60]

Libertinus was frightened by the request, but, as Gregory put it, he "came face to face with the devotedness of a mother." Libertinus dismounted his horse, "knelt down and raised his hands to heaven."[61] Then, "the boy came back to life! Libertinus took him by the hand and gave him back to his weeping mother." Gregory went on to say that it was the faith of both the mother and Libertinus that enabled "such a striking miracle" to happen. He then proceeded to tell how the gentleness and humility of Libertinus melted the heart of a harsh abbot and changed the abbot into a gentle person.[62]

For Gregory, stories of charismatic activity were by no means wonders to be gawked at for themselves alone. For him they illustrated some aspect of the Christian life or the kingdom of God. Another miracle account is about Boniface, a young boy who had grown in prayer and charity at an early age. "While he was still at home with his mother, he would sometimes leave the house and later return

---

60 Gregory the Great, *Dialogues*, (the Fathers of the Church vol. 39) p. 11.
61 Ibid., p. 11.
62 Ibid., p. 11.

without his coat or even without his shirt, for, as soon as he saw anyone in need of clothes, he would give up his own... Dialogues[63] Going to the granary one day, the mother found that her son had distributed to the poor almost all the wheat she had stored up that year for the family. The thought of having lost a whole year's food supply nearly drove her frantic. Boniface, seeing her in such distress, tried to console her as well as he knew how. But she would not listen to him. So he begged her to leave the granary. Meanwhile, he knelt down beside the small pile of what remained and prayed fervently. Then he invited his mother to come back again into the granary. It was now filled to the top with a supply of grain much greater than before. Moved to repentance by this miracle, the mother thereafter urged her son to continue giving freely, since his prayers were so quickly and abundantly answered."[64]

WINNING THE ENGLISH NATION TO CHRIST BY MIRACLES AND PREACHING

The missionaries to the north were also experiencing God's power in healing and other miracles. We know the details in part because of Gregory's own letters to them, and theirs to him. One such team consisted of the missionaries to Britain under Augustine of Canterbury who went to convert the pagan king. Their missionary message to these tribes was "how merciful Jesus, by his own agony, has redeemed the sinful world and opened the kingdom of heaven to all believers." They were winning the English nation to the Lord "by miracles and preaching," as the sixth century historian Bede put it. Gregory was jubilant about the way the Lord was working through Augustine and his missionary team. He had this to say about it. "By the shining miracles of his preachers God has brought the faith even to the extremities

---

63   Ibid., 40.

64   Ibid., 40.

of the earth. The tongue of Britain, which before could only utter barbarous sounds, has lately learned to make the alleluia resound in praise to God." To his friend Eulogius he wrote that Augustine and his companions "seemed to be imitating the powers of the apostles in the signs which they displayed." Prophetic gifts are mentioned numerous times in the Dialogues. He stated that the Spirit of Prophecy "does not always illuminate the minds of the prophets." The Lord "gives the Spirit of prophecy at some times and at other times he withdraws it. He both lifts the prophet's mind on high and yet preserves him in humility. Thus, by the gift of the Spirit, they may know what they are by God's grace, and at other times, destitute of the same Spirit, they may understand what they are of themselves."[65]

JESUS CHRIST WAS HERE!

As we have seen, Gregory placed importance on miracles. He believed, as he said in one of his sermons, "if the work of the Lord could be comprehended by reason, it would be no longer wonderful." For him, the work of miracles and the charismatic phenomena were a participation in and an imitation of, the work of Christ. In the Dialogues he stated that "every act of our Redeemer, performed through his human nature, was meant to be a pattern for our actions."[66] Another statement from the Dialogue makes a worthy conclusion to this glimpse at God's work in the late sixth century. After glimpsing a healing, Gregory states, "If any would ask you how this happened, tell him simply that the Lord Jesus Christ was here doing his work."[67]

---

[65] Gregory the Great, *The Dialogues of St. Gregory* translated by Edmund Gardner, p. 82.
[66] *Dialogues*, Westminster. 36.
[67] Ibid., 146.

Miracles, Visions and Healings Through the Centuries

Miracles, healing and visions did not end with Gregory's time. For many more centuries they imbued daily life with the wonder of the Holy Spirit.

Many of us think of reality as natural and supernatural. Supernatural events, such as healings and seeing angels break natural law. This view, though, is actually recent, from the seventeenth century on. The idea that we could observe reality from a neutral unattached stance came with the Enlightenment. People are saying today, including many scientists, that the very act of observing changes what we see. Like it or not we are in relationship with what we observe. We cannot see God or his works from the viewpoint of an unattached viewer. We are brought into relationship with him as we observe him and all he has created.

Before the Enlightenment our ancestors did not divide reality like it was divided during and after the Enlightenment. They held to a view that was more sophisticated and subtle.

Before the Enlightenment even the most amazing miracles were seen as natural. God upheld everything, each moment. Everything He does and creates is natural.

Miracles were seen as signs that provoked wonder and astonishment in people.

Our ancestors in faith viewed everything as both natural and miracle at the same time. Mountains, winds, rain, and crops for instance were seen as miraculous.

For great leaders like Augustine, everything was natural and miracle all at once. When we became too accustomed to the daily miracles, we needed special signs, contrary to the normal course of nature, but still natural, to help us to see the wondrous that surrounds us every minute. Augustine says: "God himself has created all that is wonderful in this world, the great miracles as well as the minor marvels I have mentioned, and he has included them all in that unique wonder, the miracle of miracles, the world itself."

These extraordinary signs are still from God, His gift, the action of His Spirit who activates hidden secondary causes.

Christians have saved thousands of accounts of these healings and miracles through the centuries, often firsthand accounts. While medievalists do a good job of calling them to attention, theologians write the history of faith almost as though they had not existed.

Keeping accounts of miracles was not new, it dated at least back to the fourth century. Pope Gregory the Great recounted scores of these miracles in his book, the *Dialogues*. Augustine gave us a record of healings and extraordinary miracles he witnessed in his parish in Hippo in 22nd book of that masterpiece, *The City of God*.

During the Medieval period, often when a miracle occurred there would be an investigation of the miracle, interviewing numerous witnesses, under cross examination. Thousands of these accounts have been passed on to us, in what is sometimes called the books of the miracles that contain the depositions. Sacred healing was a common event in ordinary villages as well as shrines. Both in the Age of the Church Fathers and in the Middle Ages, as medievalist Benedicta Ward put it, "miracles formed an integral part of everyday life...[They were] closely woven into the texture of Christian experience."[68]

We see today this same anticipation at the wondrous of

---

[68] Benedicta Ward, *Miracles and the Medieval Mind: Theory, Record, and Event*, 1000–1215 (The Middle Ages Series) (Philadelphia: University of Pennsylvania Press, 1987), 1–2.

Lourdes and other shrines and in shrines such as Santiago de Compostela.

Protestants show the same impulse in certain revival movements and pilgrimages to certain churches, such as Brownsville Church in Pensacola, where miraculous events are said to occur.

Visions were common in Gaul through the eighth century, not just in saints' lives but among ordinary people. Isabel Moreira's scholarly book *Dreams, Visions, and Spiritual Authority in Merovingian Gaul*, documents the prevalence of visions in this era. She writes, "A strong tradition of unrestricted access to the supernatural through dreams and visions persisted into the early middle ages..."[69]

She also notes that more and more emphasis was placed on the mystical visions of holy people and saints. As she states clearly, "By the high middle ages, visionary literature and dream narratives were at the heart of the Christian tradition." In Gaul, she says, "The texts are alive with humble, dirty and rascally inhabitants of Gaul who were apparently ennobled by divine favor."[70]

---

[69] Isabel Moreira, *Dreams, Visions, and Spiritual Authority in Merovingian Gaul* (Ithaca: Cornell University Press, 2000), 15.

[70] Ibid., 15.

CHAPTER 4

A Time of Faith

*Now is the time God comes to look for us. With arms outstretched,
we are dyed in his blood.*
—Ruteboeuf

In the next several chapters we will look at the amazing and continuous history of glossolalia prayer and expressive worship in the Age of Faith and in the centuries that immediately followed the Age of Faith.

To properly understand the history of expressive worship and jubilation, we need to understand the faith that produced the wonder that broke forth in wordless sounds and spontaneous worship. This age was the era of the cathedrals and miracles, a high-water mark in the history of the Church.

There are many common misunderstandings about the medieval world at its high point. Many tend to think of it as a time of dry philosophy and metaphysics or as a time of religious rigidity and conformity. Some think of it as an age of darkness and superstition.

Actually it was a time of tender and warm faith, an age of creative intellectual ferment, a time that produced many charismatics and charismatic movements. A look at some of the highlights of this period will give us a backdrop, a context, in which to understand the expressive worship of people in this time and in the centuries that followed.

The years from 1050-1350 were a springtime for the Christian Church. It emerged from the long night of bloody barbarian invasions to a remarkable period of life. There flourished a warm devotion to a tender and personal Jesus. Men possessed a childlike but deeply rooted faith that allowed them to discover new dimensions of human love and charity. This faith and wonder found expression in the lofty spires of cathedrals and in remarkable works of music and art. Faith in miracles, sometimes to the point of excessive credulity, abounded. It takes fertile ground to produce saints and mystics, and this fertile ground produced men of the stature of Bernard of Clairvaux and Francis. Saints were many, and nearly every city or village could claim its share of holy men and mystics who had lived there.

Wonder and praise found an outlet in expressive prayer and worship. The jubilation tradition received from the early Church continued and flourished. Though improvised jubilation was no longer a regular part of the liturgy, it remained part of the prayer experience of common people.

Rich new understandings of this and other forms of expressive prayer developed. From the fifth century until the eleventh, Europe had been overwhelmed by successive waves of barbarian invaders. First there was the wave of Germanic invasions, and then the challenge of Islam. The years between 900-1000 were particularly dark as hordes of Asiatic tribes and Scandinavian and Saracen pirates pillaged Europe.

The faithfulness of the Church during the six hundred-year barbarian night paved the way for the springtime that came to Europe in the eleventh century. Her willingness to convert barbarian tribes and barbarian princes, her faithfulness in preserving small embryos of learning and culture in

Christian communities, the openness of many of their children to seek greater union with God in contemplative prayer—all paved the way for this springtime.

This three-hundred-year springtime produced the universities and the great works of scholastic theology and perhaps, more importantly, succeeded in humanizing and Christianizing a whole society. The Church historian H. Daniel-Rops, in his work on this period, *Cathedral and Crusade*, says: "For three long centuries...society enjoyed what may be considered the richest, most fruitful, most harmonious epoch in all the history of Europe, an epoch which may be likened to spring after the barbarian winter."[71]

CHRISTIANITY WITH A HUMAN FACE

The movements of Francis, Bernard and Dominic spoke of a love of a very human Jesus. St. Bernard, who lived in the twelfth century and perhaps influenced the popular devotion of the Age of Faith more than any one person, could say: "Hail, Jesus, whom I love. Thou knowest how I long to be nailed with thee to the cross. Give thyself to me Draw me wholly to thee, and say to me: 'I heal thee, I forgive thee...' I embrace thee in a surge of love."[72]

St. Francis of Assisi, who was more than anything else a "friend of Jesus," along with the brothers who followed him, sent this devotion to Jesus ringing through the cities and villages of Europe.

The God-man was not simply Christ or the incarnation or the "Word made flesh." The name for Him that was most loved was His tender, personal name "Jesus." Devotion to the name of Jesus was an important facet of faith in this time.

---

71 H. Daniel-Rops, *Cathedral and Crusade* (New York: E.P. Dutton and Co. Inc., 1957), p. 2. Many of the concepts in this chapter are taken from Daniel-Rops' treatment of this era.

72 Quoted in Ibid, p. 48.

People commonly prayed and sang little poems, sometimes known as "jubilations," that included a repetition of the name of Jesus with a short descriptive phrase.

The word that was most used in these descriptions was "dulcis" or "sweet." St. Bernard's words tremble with tenderness as he repeats the name of Jesus. He says to his monks: "Your affection for your Lord Jesus should be both tender and intimate."[73]

In a sermon on the healing power of Jesus, Bernard sees healing for both body and soul in the name of Jesus. He says: "What a splendor radiated from that light, dazzling the eyes of the crowd when Peter uttered the name that strengthened the feet and ankle of the cripple, and gave light to many eyes that were spiritually blind! Did not the words shoot like a flame when he said: 'In the name of Jesus Christ of Nazareth, arise and walk.' But the name of Jesus is more than light, it is also food. Do you not feel increase of strength as often as you remember it? What other name can so enrich the man who meditates? ...

"Write what you will, I shall not relish it unless it tells of Jesus. Talk or argue about what you will, I shall not relish it if you exclude the name of Jesus. Jesus to me is honey in the mouth, music in the ear, a song in the heart. Again, it is a medicine. Does one of us feel sad? Let the name of Jesus come into his heart, from there let it spring to his mouth, so that shining like the dawn it may dispel all darkness and make a cloudless sky."[74]

One of the most moving poems of this period was Bernard's "Rhythmical Jubilation on the name of Jesus." This poem soars to poetic heights over the name of Jesus. Here are a

---

73 St. Bernard of Clairvaux, *On the Song of Songs*, tr. by Kilian Walsh (Spencer, Massachusetts: Cistercian Publications, 1971) vol. I, p. 150.

74 Ibid, p. 110.

few stanzas from this long poem:

> No sweeter soul can soothe the ear, The voice no sweeter song can sing, No sweeter thought the soul can cheer, Than Jesus, Son of heaven's King. The love of Jesus brings delight.[75]

Many others besides Bernard wrote similar words on the name of Jesus. Hymns such as the *Jesu, Dulcis Memoria* (Jesus, The Sweet Remembrance of You) were the songs of the average peasant and townsman.

The writings of the Franciscans and other groups are also full of these devotions to the name of Jesus. The writings of a fourteenth-century English preacher and mystic, Richard Rolle, are also full of this same devotion. He says: "I cannot pray, I cannot meditate, but in sounding the name of Jesus, I savor no joy that is not mingled with Jesus. Wheresoever I be, wheresoever I sit, whatsoever I do, the thought of the savor of the name of Jesus never leaves my mind... Verily the name of Jesus is in my mind a joyous song and heavenly music in mine ear, and in my mouth a honeyed sweetness."[76]

This devotion to the name of Jesus bears remarkable similarity to the constant use of this name in Pentecostalism. Perhaps it marks a shift in emphasis from Jesus the concept to Jesus the person.

A Renewed Human Love

The emphasis on the human side of God went hand in hand with a renewed emphasis on human love.

For the spiritual writer of the Age of Faith, warm love of

---

[75] St. Bernard of Clairvaux, *Sermons for the Seasons and Principal Festivals* (Westminster, Md.: The Carroll Press, 1950), pp. 447-456.

[76] C. C. Heseltine, *Selected Works of Richard Rolle* (New York: Longmans, Green and Co., 1930), p. 81.

God and warm love of one's Christian brother or sister were inseparable. Though it may surprise us, one of the centers for this emphasis on strongly felt Christian love was the monastery, especially the Cistercian monasteries.

The guiding light of this movement was St. Bernard of Clairvaux. Perhaps more than anyone, he sums up in his person the medieval ideal of human love and tenderness. As a young man of twenty two, Bernard entered the Cistercian order.

During his lifetime he "swayed Christendom as never did a holy man before or after him,"[77] as one medieval scholar put it. He led preaching missions all over Europe, helped decide secular disputes, and introduced many new reforms to the Church.

He could be strong and bold in proclaiming his opinions. At the same time he was a man of incredible tenderness. This tenderness even shone in his outward appearance. His first biographer says of him: "Because he was a helper for the Holy Spirit, God made his body to conform to his mission. In his human appearance there was a certain grace—a spiritual grace, not an earthly one. A brightness not of earth shone in his facial expression; there was an angelic purity in his eyes, a dove-like simplicity. The beauty of the inner man was so great that it would burst forth in visible tokens, and the outer man would seem bathed from the store of inward purity and overflowing grace."[78]

This tenderness of Bernard for his fellow men can be seen in his letters and in his sermons. He told his monks: "Let us love affectionately, discreetly, intensely."[79]

---

77 Taylor, *The Medieval Mind*, vol. I, 392.
78 Taylor, 408.
79 Bernard, *Song of Songs*, p. 150.

His affection could be deeply human, as is seen in a sermon he interrupted when the thought came to him of his beloved brother Gerard who had recently died.

One morning in chapel, as he was teaching from a passage in the Song of Songs, the thought of his deceased brother Gerard came to his mind, causing him to pause. To the astonishment of those present he broke out into tears and continued: "You tell me not to weep? My bowels are torn out; shall I have no feeling? Nay, if I suffer, I do so with my whole being. I am not made of stone; my heart is not a heart of bronze. I confess my woe. It is carnal, you say? I know that well, for I know that I am a creature of flesh and blood, sold under sin, delivered unto death, and subject to suffering. What would you? I am not insensible to grief; I have a horror of death, both for myself and for those I love; Gerard has left me, and I am in pain; I am wounded unto death."[80]

His letters are full of expressions of affection. One was to Robert, a young man who left Bernard's monastery at Clairvaux when he was still a young man. A good part of the reason was the severity of the way Bernard treated him at the monastery. Bernard one day realized he had made a mistake with Robert and wrote a letter asking for his forgiveness.

According to his biographer Bernard was so anxious to set the matter right that he stole out of the monastery, accompanied by his secretary William, in order to write a letter to Robert. While he was busy dictating the letter to Robert a rainstorm broke on them. William wanted to stop. "Go ahead and write. Don't worry; it's God work," said Bernard. So William kept on writing in the midst of the rain, but not a drop fell on him or on the parchment on which he was writing, such was the power of love which

---

80 Daniel-Rops, *Cathedral*, p. 87.

dictated the letter.[81]

Here are some extracts from that letter: "You are right. I admit it. I am writing to you not to argue with you but to end argument...I pass over what happened; I do not ask why or how it happened. I don't discuss faults, I don't quibble over the circumstances, I have no memory for injuries. What I speak to you is what is on my heart. How terribly sad I am that I am without you and do not see you; that I am not living with you, with whom to live would be life...I don't ask why you have gone away; I complain only that you do not return...It surely was my fault that you left us. I was too strict with you although you were just a youth...I never meant it harshly. Come back and you will find me changed. Before you feared me as a religious superior; but now you will embrace me as a friend and companion."[82]

Here is one of hundreds of accounts to experiences of the Holy Spirit and wondrous in the age of the Fathers and Mothers. In this case it is an eyewitness account in the biography of Ambrose by his close friend Paulinus:

> "when he (Ambrose) was dictating the forty-third psalm, with me carefully taking it down, a fire like a small shield suddenly covered his head, and little by little entered his mouth, just as a person enters his home. After this, his face turned white as snow, but soon regained its usual appearance...I, you may be sure, straightway reported what I had seen to the honorable deacon Castus, under whose care I was then living. But he, filled with the grace of God, pointed out to me from the passage of the Acts of the Apostles that I had seen in the bishop the coming of

---

81 As quoted in Taylor, Vol.1, p. 411.

82 This excerpt from Bernard's letter is adapted into contemporary English from a more archaic English. It is found in Taylor, vol.1, p. 395-396.

the Holy Spirit."[83]

Aelred of Rievaulx, an early Cistercian, makes the point in his treatise on spiritual friendship that knowing a friend deeply can help us know Christ. For him the embraces of friends help us to embrace God. He says: "In this way, beginning with the love with which he has embraced his friend, and rising up to the love with Christ, he will with great happiness enjoy the delight of the friendship of friendships (i.e. friendship with God)."[84]

SAINTS AND MYSTICS

This was the era of the Church that produced Francis of Assisi, Dominic, Bernard and St. Thomas Aquinas. The real heroes of this age were the seekers after God, the mystics. Mysticism is that state of love in which a man "touches" and "tastes" God in almost tangible ways.

Mysticism involved radical transformation. In this transformation men were drawn intensely close to God and their fellow men. The inner journey a man goes on during this transformation involves facing and coming to grips with his own sin and selfishness and allowing the tender grace of God to forgive and transform him in radical ways.

Today we think of mystics as men and women who are somehow apart from the world, apart from people. This was not the case in the medieval world. Mystics like Francis and Bernard were intimately tied to their fellow Christians and displayed an extraordinary capacity for friendship. Certainly there were times of solitude in their lives, but the overwhelming witness of the medieval mystics was that they were men and women who very much rubbed elbows

---

[83] Paulinus, *The Life of Ambrose, found in Early Christian Biographies*, trans. Roy J.Deferrari (Washington, DC : Catholic University of America Press, 1952), 59.

[84] As quoted in William Johnston, *Silent Music* (New York: Harper and Row, 1974), p. 148.

with their fellows and in doing so brought them closer to God.

THE COMMON BELIEVER

This pull toward God was also felt by common believers who prayed much more then than today. Ordinary Christians often possessed the prayer of tears and engaged in contemplative prayer. H. Daniel-Rops says: "Medieval Christians, however, were not content with oral prayer alone. Mystical writers explain that there is another and more interior form, which they describe as 'mental prayer'; nor is it uncommon to find, even in such profane works as the *Chansons de Geste*, the hero 'praying in silence.' Geoffrey of Vendome (d. 1132) even speaks of the 'prayer of tears,' which seems to have been widely practiced."[85]

Scripture played an important role in the faith of the common believer. The Bible as a whole was familiar to all. According to H. Daniel-Rops, "the first and most fundamental (characteristic of medieval religion)…was the influence of Holy Scripture."[86]

One of the signs that Christians were thoroughly conversant with Scripture is the constant use of scriptural themes in the stained-glass windows of cathedrals and churches. These helped bring the Bible alive to both literate and illiterate alike.

Groups of wandering preachers such as the Franciscans brought the stories of the Bible and the truths of the Christian faith to the common man, and breathed into them a great human tenderness and a warm emotionality. For those who could read, the Bible was readily available in Latin. Educated laymen who could not read Latin had

---

85 Daniel-Rops, *Cathedral*, 56.
86 Daniel-Rops, *Cathedral*, 44.

translations of books and parts of Scripture. Those who are familiar with medieval devotional writings know how deeply the writers drank from the wellspring of Scripture.

Miracles and the Charismatic Element

One of the characteristics of the Age of Faith was a widespread belief in miracles. Says one medieval scholar: "(This) was a genuine piety of a people who lived in a constant state of mystical exaltation, who believed passionately in miracles, and who were ever ready to make great sacrifices to support and defend their religion."[87]

Accounts of healings and other miracles are plentiful in medieval literature, especially in the lives of the saints. Today people hesitate to believe in the charismatic element, the wondrous element. The opposite was true in the Age of Faith. The people of this time possessed a near childlike credulity; they were almost too ready to believe.

Most people today are aware that accounts of miracles occurred in the lives of the saints. Yet there are significant accounts of miracles occurring in more ordinary circumstances, among more ordinary people. The account of the building of the Cathedral of Chartres is full of stories of dozens of healings that took place in the midst of healing services that were held while the cathedral was being built. We will look at this account of the building of Chartres more closely in the next chapter. Gabler's history of Burgundy describes a healing service as part of the Church Council. He says: "Then were innumerable sick folk healed in those conclaves of holy men; and, lest men should think lightly of mere bursten skin or rent flesh in the straightening of arms and legs, much blood flowed forth also when the crooked

---

87 *The Mind of the Middle Ages*, (New York: Alfred A. Knopf, 1954), p. 100.

limbs were restored, which gave faith to the rest who might have doubted."[88]

This belief in miracles led to an atmosphere of creativity as well as to achievements in science, literature and the other arts. Says H. Daniel-Rops: "Belief in the supernatural is certainly one of the most admirable qualities of the medieval mentality. It exalted man by assuring him he could rise above himself and attain to greatness. It caused him also to dwell in that atmosphere of poetry and wonder from which the arts derived considerable benefit."[89]

DEVOTION TO THE HOLY SPIRIT

Devotion to the Holy Spirit also played a part in the faith of the medieval believer. One of the ways of looking at miracles and charismatic phenomena was still a part of the work of the Holy Spirit, similar to the charismatic theology of St. Paul in 1 Corinthians 12-14 where he speaks of the Holy Spirit as the giver of spiritual gifts such as prophecy, miracles and healing.

This is well brought out in a remarkable sermon by St. Bernard written for Pentecost. In this sermon he urges his listeners to seek a further experience of the moving of the Holy Spirit. He says: "The Spirit communicates himself for the working of miracles in signs and prodigies and other supernatural operations which he effects by the hands of whomsoever he pleases, renewing the wonders of bygone times, so that the events of the present may confirm our belief as to those of the past."[90]

This was a time when hymns to the Holy Spirit such as

---

88 Jay Williams, *Life in the Middle Ages* (Cambridge, Cambridge University Pres,1967) p.6.
89 Daniel-Rops, *Cathedral*, 35.
90 St. Bernard, *Sermons for the Seasons*, pp. 315-316.

Veni, Creator (Come, Creator Spirit) and *Veni, Sancte Spiritus* (Come, O Holy Spirit) were popular. Bernard and others spoke of an experience of the Holy Spirit beyond that of salvation. While they saw this as an experience of the Spirit beyond baptism and confirmation, we should not too readily assume that this experience is exactly identical with what modern-day charismatics call "baptism in the Spirit." There are many close similarities; however, both views of receiving the Spirit suggest a further dynamic of the Spirit's operation beyond that of a minimal Christian life. For medieval writers on devotion, this experience of the Spirit was a time of growing spontaneity, a further giving of oneself to God and a greater docility toward the inspirations of the Spirit. Both modern-day charismatics and the faithful of the medieval period see an important place for a further work of the Spirit in the Christian life. Bernard says in his sermon on "Ways That the Holy Ghost Is Communicated": "He is given finally to fill us with fervor, when, breathing with power upon the hearts of the perfect, he enkindles within them a strong fire of charity... We have all, I think, received the Spirit unto salvation, but not to all has he been given unto fervor. In fact, only very few appear to be filled with this spirit of fervor, very few show any desire to obtain it. We are content with our own cramped littleness, and make no endeavor to rejoice in or at least to aspire to the liberty of spirit which that Spirit confers."

Bernard then moves into a touching call for a new Pentecost, a fresh coming of the Holy Spirit: "Let us pray, dearest brethren, that in us may be accomplished the days of Pentecost, the days of remission, the days of exultation, the days of the true jubilee."[91]

This experience of the Holy Spirit creates greater love.

---

91   Ibid., pp. 315-316.

Bernard's friend William of St. Thierry says that people should receive an experience of the Holy Spirit that "not only enlightens unto knowledge, but inflames to love."

Intellectual and Cultural Accomplishments

This was also a time of great cultural and intellectual accomplishments. The Age of Faith produced great contributions to culture that have remained to enrich each era since. It was then that the universities were founded and the beginnings of Western literature emerged. Solid work in philosophy ballasted the religion of revelation. This was the time that lofty cathedrals rose as a witness to faith, the time of frescoes and polyphonic music. Fresh breezes blew in the realms of political and scientific thought, and the foundations of modern science were laid in this period.

There is a common belief that the medieval period was a time of rigid religious conformity. Scholars of this period know how false this notion is. On the contrary, this was a time of creative theological ferment. In the universities the greatest minds confronted one in sometimes passionate arguments. The encounter with the philosophies of Islam, the Greek Church and the rediscovery of many of the Fathers and classical thought led to a time of thinking through the entire Christian faith. It was during this period that the remarkable systems of men like St. Thomas Aquinas and St. Bonaventure were produced. This rethinking of Christianity was stimulated by the Church being put in greater touch with the Fathers of the Church.

Transformed Society

During these three hundred years we see a vital Christianity that not only changed the Church but also changed society. Certainly everything was not perfect, but when we compare the society of the Age of Faith with what came before, the society of barbarian tribes and Roman society, we can see what a profound change the Christian Church and the Christian Gospel worked on Europe.

Roman writers tended to see love as a grasping, at times erotic, selfish emotion. The Age of Faith, in contrast, saw love as warm, strong, and self-giving. Roman society placed little value on human life. Infants were often abandoned to die on mountain tops; men were sent to die for sport in the arena.

In Christian Europe of the Middle Ages human life had been given eternal dignity and worth. While the Age of Faith had its faults, it bore witness to the fact that the Christian Gospel, lived in fullness, changes society. This change, this transformation, came about to a large extent because of the pull of faith, the pull of a charismatic faith that had room for saints and mystics, for miracles, for the wondrous in all its dimensions.

No Utopia

The Christian Church has at no time in its history been a Utopia, a "little heaven" without problems. As we can tell from the letters in the New Testament, the apostolic Church certainly had its share of problems. Among them were some of the more scandalous sins such as incest, adultery, bitter factional fighting, and backbiting. It also had its glory, its love and its sense of wonder. The same was true of the Church of the Middle Ages. It was a time of very vital faith, perhaps the most vital time of faith the Church has ever known, but it too had its problems. There was a marked anti-Semitism, and the behavior of a great many of the Crusaders was anything but commendable. No small number of bishops and even a few popes were hardly worthy of their positions, and at times disgraced them.

The person who cannot accept that the wheat and weeds grow together in the Church, the person who wants to separate the good from the "not so good" and have a "pure" Church, has failed to understand the mystery of the Church. The mystery of the Church is that the perfect love of God comes to men through clay pots. Through the sin, the wounds, the mistakes of Christ's people, God's perfect love comes.

Still, for all the faults of this time, a multitude of people experienced a vigorous Christianity. The Gospel was the constitution for society. It was a society that felt it was "dyed" in Christ's blood, as one poet of the times, Ruteboef, stated: Now is the time God comes to look for us. With arms outstretched; we are dyed in his blood."[92]

These words from H. Daniel-Rops perhaps make a worthy conclusion to this glimpse of medieval faith: "So long as men believed firmly in the Gospel teaching, society was dominated by the Christian faith. Practically no aspect of the Middle Ages can be properly understood except by reference to Christian principles.

"Everyone felt himself to be 'dyed in Christ's blood'; every facet of human life, indeed, bore the sign of the cross."[93]

---

92 Daniel-Rops, *Cathedral*, p. 33.
93 Daniel-Rops, *Cathedral*, p. 75.

CHAPTER 5

THE MIDDLE AGES

Nothing more imitates the state of heavenly glory than Praises to God spontaneously sung.
—St. Bernard of Clairvaux

The age that produced the cathedrals and inspired scholastic theology was a time of spontaneous worship. This high-water mark of Catholic Christianity was a time when ordinary Christians expressed their wonder in much the same way that modern charismatics express theirs—by praying aloud without words and singing inspired songs. This tradition continued for several hundred years after the end of the Middle Ages—the period in which so many of the aspects of Catholic Christianity were formed, the time of Francis, Aquinas and Dominic.

A CONTINUING TRADITION

The jubilation tradition of the early Church continued into the Middle Ages. So did other forms of spontaneous prayer and worship. These traditions grew in richness, as faith as a whole grew in richness during this period. Though spontaneous jubilation was no longer an expected part of the plain-song of the Church, it was still a common way of praying.

Taking on a more spontaneous character, the experience of jubilation more and more included spontaneous body movements and dance-like gestures. It could still be the prayer of ordinary Christians until at least the end of the Middle Ages. Jubilation also played a significant part in the lives of mystics and saints. Let us look at the two types of jubilation that developed during this period.

ORDINARY JUBILATION

As in the age of the Fathers we find no clear-cut distinction between the styles of jubilation. Still certain classifications are helpful.

Ordinary jubilation was the more common form of jubilation. It was a singing or speaking of wordless phrases. It could be a form of individual prayer as with some of the early Franciscan brothers or it could be a group experience of singing and praying under the influence of the Holy Spirit. Several accounts mention thousands of people at a time harmonizing in this manner.

In this period the word jubilation could also be used to describe singing improvised songs in one's own language under the inspiration of the Holy Spirit.

MYSTICAL JUBILATION

Mystical jubilation, as we have seen in the chapter on jubilation in the Fathers, was an exuberant form of jubilation that often included various sorts of outward manifestations besides wordless sounds. During the Middle Ages mystical jubilation became a significant part of most spiritual traditions. Writers on mystical prayer such as St. John of the Cross, St. Teresa of Avila, St. Bernard of Clairvaux, and many others, mention it. It is experienced and described in varying ways. The accounts of the lives of saints and mystics are also full of this type of prayer.

Spiritual Inebriation

Jubilation was, at times, called "spiritual inebriation." The use of the phrase is derived from the book of Acts where on the day of Pentecost, when the disciples are exuberantly praising God after the coming of the Holy Spirit, they are accused of being drunk "with new wine" (Acts 2:13). Peter answers this charge by saying that they are not drunk and then describes the outpouring of the Spirit (Acts 2:15-21).

There is also the passage in Ephesians in which Paul urges his hearers not to be drunk with wine but to be "filled with the Spirit" (Eph. 5:18). Then in the same passage he proceeds to suggest that they be filled with the Spirit in "addressing one another in psalms and hymns and spiritual songs, singing and making melody to the Lord with all your heart" (Eph. 5:19-20).

In the use of the term "spiritual inebriation" or "spiritual drunkenness" one can sense real identification with New Testament passages on the exuberant worship of the disciples at Pentecost and the spiritual song of the New Testament.

Other Forms of Expressive Worship

Sometimes jubilation is described by other words, and sometimes words other than jubilation are used to describe the exuberant worship. The tradition of sighs, shouts and other forms of spontaneity that we saw in the Fathers is preserved.

Close Relationship with Tongues

In the medieval period we can see an even closer resemblance to the tongues of the New Testament and the tongues of the modern-day Pentecostal movement. One highly renowned scholar of medieval culture and mysticism, Evelyn Underhill, has done perhaps the most significant work on understanding the jubilation of the medieval period.

She suggests a close kinship between the jubilation of the medieval period and the tongues of the New Testament. She says: "Richard Rolle, Ruysbroeck, and others, have left us vivid descriptions of the jubilus, which seems to have been, in their day, like the closely-related 'speaking with tongues' in the early Church, a fairly common expression of intense religious excitement."[94]

In certain passages in Franciscan literature we find the sounds of certain jubilations actually written out. These descriptions are amazingly like descriptions of present-day glossolalia within Pentecostalism.

THEOLOGIANS AND SCHOLARS

Jubilation was not simply the experience of peasant folk and a few saints and mystics; it was described and probably experienced by many of the major theologians and intellectual figures of the Middle Ages. The theologians and scholars had a great sense that jubilation was a heritage they received from the early Church. They often quote and paraphrase the Fathers on jubilation, and at the same time they add new insight to the work of the Fathers on jubilation.

A good way to find out what the understanding of a word

---

[94] "But these acute emotional reactions, often accompanied by eccentric outward behaviour, are a normal episode in the early development of many mystics; upon whom the beauty and wonder of the new world of spirit now perceived by them and the Presence that fills it, have often an almost intoxicating effect. Richard Rolle, Ruysbroeck, and others have left us vivid descriptions of the *jubilus, which seems to have been in their day, like the closely-related 'speaking with tongues' in the early Church, a fairly common expression of intense religious excitement.*" Evelyn Underhill, *Jacopone da Todi* (New York: E.P. Dutton and Co., 1919), pp. 77-78.

or concept in a particular age happens to be is to turn to a dictionary. Toward the late Middle Ages, in 1490, we have an excellent description of jubilation given in a Spanish-Latin dictionary, the *Universal Vocabulario*. It paraphrases Gregory on jubilation when it says that jubilation is a joy that one cannot express in words, yet a joy which cannot be contained. The dictionary then adds some fresh insights: "Jubilation is when such a great joy is conceived in the heart that it cannot be expressed in words, yet neither can it be concealed or hidden. It cannot be expressed in words... It manifests itself with very happy gestures... The voice is excited to song."[95]

In this definition we see a much greater emphasis placed on gestures than in patristic definitions. It seems that the expression of joy by means of the voice and the expression of joy by means of the body—in lively gestures—form a whole, a unity.

One of the things that one senses in the writings of various periods of Church history on jubilation is that jubilation was almost never controversial. Parts of the Church's doctrine that are controversial or disputed such as the Trinity, the person of Christ, the Eucharist, and the Assumption receive very precise definitions and have quite a bit written about them. In a sense they become written in stone and receive a prominent place in the literature of the Church. Other practices and doctrines that are not as controversial, but perhaps are nearly as important, do not receive the same sort of definition and usually don't find as prominent a place in the theological literature of the Church. An example of this is the doctrine of brotherly love. Christian love is certainly at the core of the faith, yet if you look on the shelves of the systematic theology section in a library you will find only

---

95 *Universal Vocabulario En Latin ye En Romance*, Reproduction Facsimilar De La Edicion De Sevilla, 1490 (Madrid: Comision Permanente De La Asociacion De Academias De La Lengua Espanola, 1967), vol. I, col. *ccxxvii*.

a handful of books that define and describe Christian love at any length. This is because the idea that Christian should love Christian is commonly accepted by most Christians, whatever their theological or denominational background. The idea that Christians should love other Christians has almost never been disputed in the history of the Church. The references that one finds to brotherly love are, for the most part in devotional literature, biographical literature—the folk literature of the faith. The same is true for jubilation. Hardly anywhere in the references to jubilation in the Fathers or in the Middle Ages is it suggested that jubilation is controversial.

The places that one finds references to jubilation are primarily in the folk-literature—the literature on mysticism and the literature on the ordinary life of the people.

We do not have long theological definitions of jubilation in the Middle Ages in the same way we do of doctrines such as the Trinity. There is a wealth of literature on jubilation found in the mystical writings and the medieval chronicles—the things that describe the more daily life of faith. Yet we do have significant references to jubilation by the significant scholars of this period. They knew and experienced this form of prayer. We find those references to jubilation, however, in such places as their devotional writings and their sermons and biblical commentaries. For these theologians also were men of fervent faith, and in their writings in which they discuss devotion and inspire to faith we have references to jubilation.

St. Thomas Aquinas

The best known theologian of this period was St. Thomas Aquinas. His work has been the major theological influence in the Catholic Church in the following centuries. We tend to think of dry metaphysics and dusty volumes when we think of St. Thomas, but he was also a man of faith. His mystical work such as *Pange Lingua and Lauda, Sion* present a different Aquinas than the one most people are familiar with—an Aquinas who was in love with a human Jesus. It is said that his sermons brought congregations to tears. He deals with jubilation primarily in his commentary on Psalms, a usual place for more devotional writing.

In his commentary on Psalm 32 (Vulgate numbering) he suggests that jubilation is the new song that Christians sing because of their renewal in grace. Jubilation is a song that expresses the mystical, the wondrous aspect of the Christian life: "That man truly sings in jubilation who sings about the good things of glory."

For him "the jubilus is an inexpressible joy which is not able to be expressed in words but even still the voice declares this vast expanse of joy (without words)."[96]

For Thomas the things that the voice expresses are the things that are beyond words, are the good things of glory. Continuing the passage on jubilation, he says: "Moreover the things which are not able to be expressed, they are the good things of glory."[97]

Again in his commentary on Psalm 46 (47 in Hebrew Bible) Thomas takes up the idea that jubilation is an expression of the good things of God that go beyond words. He says: "Jubilation is an unspeakable joy, which one cannot keep silent; yet neither can it be expressed (in words). The reason that (this joy) cannot be expressed in words is that it is beyond comprehension. ...Such is the goodness of God that it cannot be expressed (in words), and even if it could be expressed (in words), it could only imperfectly be

---

96   St. Thomas Aquinas, *In Psalterium David*, in Ps. 32.

97   Aquinas, *In Psalterium*, in Ps. 32, 3.

expressed."⁹⁸

Thus we see in Aquinas a sense that part of our knowledge of God is beyond conception, beyond conceptual language. Many of the good things of God are too wonderful to be expressed in words. Yet they are so wonderful that the Christian cannot keep silent.

But even jubilation is only a foretaste. For him jubilation was the praise of the apostles when Jesus ascended into heaven. For him there were two types of praises at the ascension— the praise of angels and the praise of the apostles.

The angels who had full comprehension, full knowledge of God could i praise perfectly. But human beings, whose knowledge of God was imperfect, could only jubilate. Jubilation, therefore, even though it was incomplete, even though it was only a foretaste, seems to have been the best way that men could enter into the praise of God.⁹⁹

BONAVENTURE

Next to St. Thomas Aquinas the theological works of St. Bonaventure were the most influential of the medieval period. Bonaventure's writings reflect both the rigor of a competent theologian and the simple love of a mystic. His writings are filled with a sense of wonder at the mystery of God and of God's creation.

Bonaventure was a second-generation Franciscan and he wrote one of the most beautiful biographies of Francis.

---

98 Aquinas, *In Psalterium*, in Ps. 46, 1.

99 "This jubilus is an immense joy. Now this jubilus indicates imperfect knowledge. There were two types of singing at the ascension of Christ, that is, that of the apostles and that of the angels. The apostles had imperfect knowledge of God and therefore jubilation from the joy of Christ ascending into glory was important (lit. pertained). Angels were also present, and they had perfect knowledge (of God). Therefore jubilation was not important to them." Aquinas, *In Psalterium*, in Ps. 46, 3.

Bonaventure knows the tradition on jubilation. He quotes Gregory, saying that it is an "inexpressible joy of mind which is not able to be hidden nor to be expressed; nevertheless it is betrayed by certain movements."

For Bonaventure it was the joy of the apostles at the ascension of Christ. It is like the joyful expressions of a bridegroom "not being able to express the cheerfulness of his mind, however perceiving it about himself."[100] Again we see another profoundly human analogy, that of a bridegroom expressing his joy.

Perhaps above all else Bonaventure was a mystic and a theologian of mysticism. Jubilation played a role in his theory of mysticism. Jubilation is particularly strong just before close union with God. In his *Triple Way*, one of his major works on mysticism, he makes this clear. First the soul is cleansed through sorrow, tears, etc. Then a perfecting of the soul comes through praise, thanksgiving and jubilation. He says: "Perfecting through gratitude implies an awareness that rises to a hymn of thanksgiving for the quality of graces that are offered, a joy that rises to jubilation for the value of the gifts we have received, and a delight that culminates in an embrace because of the Giver's bounty."[101]

JEAN GERSON

Jean Gerson was one of the top scholars of the Middle Ages. As rector of the University of Paris, he made many contributions to higher education. He was also a popular preacher whose sermons were enjoyed by the masses.

He describes a particularly exuberant form of jubilation, contrasting the jubilation of the devout Christians with the

---

100 St. Bonaventure, *In Ps.* 46, 3.

101 St. Bonaventure, *The Triple Way* as found in *The Works of Bonaventure*, translated from the Latin by Jose de Vinck (Paterson, N.J.: St. Anthony Guild Press, 1960), p. 90.

unruly noise of the streets and theaters. Christian jubilation came out of a deep experience of the Lord's joy and can come during ecstasy: "The hilarity of the devout...in a certain wonderful and unexplainable sweetness seizes the mind...so that now it does not contain itself. There happens some sort of a spasm, ecstasy or departure...The mind springs forth; it leaps, or dances by means of the gestures of the body, which are comely, and then it jubilates in an inexpressible way... The praise is pleasant, the praise is comely, since the purity of the heart sings along with the voice."[102] So for Gerson jubilation is a pure joy of the heart that manifests itself in the body through song and spontaneous bodily gestures.

OTHER THEOLOGIANS AND SCHOLARS

Other renowned theologians of the medieval period, such as Albertus Magnus and Peter Lombard, also describe jubilation in similar ways.

THE EARLY FRANCISCANS

In the first part of the thirteenth century, in the thriving trading town of Assisi, Italy, a young man began to act strangely. Normally a likeable, fun-loving playboy, he began to spend a lot of time away from friends and family. The people of the town noticed the fresh bright glint in his eye and suspected that he was in love and about to marry. "Are you going to take a wife?" they asked him. "Yes," he answered. "I am marrying a bride more beautiful and more noble than any you have ever seen." The young man was Francis Bernadone, and the bride he was taking, as the townspeople were later to find out, was "the Kingdom of heaven," "the life of the Gospel."[103]

---

102 Jean Gerson, *Oevres Completes*, vol. V. p. 284.

103 *Early Franciscan Classics* (Paterson, New Jersey: St. Anthony Guild Press, 1962), p. 15.

This was St. Francis of Assisi. Many of us have misconceptions about him. We tend to think only of his love for animals. For many he is known only as the saint that is found in birdbaths. Francis was much more than a lover of animals. Francis was most of all a "friend of Jesus." Francis and his followers had a deep, devotion to Jesus. An early biographer says of Francis: "He was always taken up with Jesus: he ever carried Jesus in his heart, Jesus on his lips, Jesus in his ears, Jesus in his eyes, Jesus in his hands, Jesus in all his members."[104]

The simple love and joy of Francis was to change the Church. Through him the Lord built a community that was to touch countless thousands before his death and millions more in the centuries to come. Within a few years of his conversion thousands of people had joined Francis' order. They filtered throughout the known world preaching the simple message of the Gospel.

These early Franciscans had a strong sense of community. God became close in the presence of a brother or sister. Francis' first biographer, Thomas of Celano, describes their sense of love for one another: "What affection for the holy companionship of their fellows flourished among them! Whenever they came together at a place, or met along the road, and exchanged the customary greeting, there rebounded between them a dart of spiritual affection, scattering over all their devotion the seed of true love. And how they showed it! Innocent embraces, gentle tenderness, 'a holy kiss,' delightful converse, modest laughter, a joyous countenance, a sound eye, a humble heart, 'a soothing tongue,' 'a mild answer,' unity of purpose, a ready devotedness, and an unwearied hand to help."[105]

What a breathtaking description of community! The wonder

---
[104] Ibid., p. 119.

[105] Ibid., pp. 43-44.

that they found in Jesus and in creation they also found in their fellow human beings. Their constant prayer led them into a wondering celebration of their brothers and sisters.

The embrace of peace could be a form of prayer. An example of this is the legend of the meeting of King Louis of France and Brother Giles. As soon as they met, "both of them hastened to embrace each other, kneeling together... as though they had been intimate friends for a long time." Giles later explained this embrace to the brothers, saying: "

"In the moment when we embraced, the light of divine wisdom revealed his heart to me and mine to him... For if we had wanted to explain with the help of our voices what we felt in our hearts, we could not have done so because of the defect of human language, which cannot clearly express the secret mysteries of God except by mystic symbols."[106] The source of this wonder which they felt toward their Lord, one another and all of creation was prayer. They were constantly praying, both together and alone. They prayed on hilltops, in abandoned churches, along the streets and roads. They often struggled in prayer with sighs and tears.

Their prayer and their praise could be exuberant and expressive, Francis loved loud praise. Once a certain brother was walking along the street carrying a bag of alms, and "as he walked he was cheerfully singing God's praises in a loud voice...Francis heard him and at once went out to meet him with the greatest fervor and joy. He ran up to him on the road and joyfully kissed the shoulder on which he was carrying a bag with alms...And he told the brothers, 'this is how I want a friar of mine to go out and return with alms: happy, joyful, and praising God.'" [107]

---

106 *The Little Flowers of St. Francis*, translated by Raphael Brown (Garden City, New York: Doubleday, 1958), pp. 122-123.

107 *St. Francis of Assisi: his life and writings as Recorded by his Contemporaries* (London: Mobray)p. 39.

Jubilation was, it seems, a very important way of praying for these early Franciscans. It is described a number of times, and in some places it is equated with contemplation. It could be a form of private prayer or a form of public prayer. Generally it was the speaking of wordless phrases as prayer or the spontaneous singing of wordless phrases or inspired songs.

One quaint story from the *Little Flowers* illustrates the way jubilation may have been prayed. The words of a jubilus are actually written out. It gives us an example of the part jubilation played in private prayer and what it might have sounded like: "And Brother Masseo remained so filled with the grace of the desired virtue of humility and with the light of God that from then on he was in jubilation all the time. And often when he was praying…he would make a jubilus that sounded like the cooing of a gentle dove 'Ooo–Ooo–Ooo.' And with a joyful expression, he would remain in contemplation in that way… Brother James of Fallerone asked him why he didn't change the intonation in his jubilation. And he (Masseo) answered very joyfully: 'Because when we have found all that is good in one thing, it is not necessary to change the intonation.'"[108]

Jubilation could be joyful, inspired song. Francis is described as breaking out into inspired songs. There is also allusion to spiritual inebriation in some of these accounts. "Intoxicated by love and compassion for Christ, Blessed Francis sometimes used to act like this. For the sweetest

---

[108] I have included the Italian version. "Frate Masseo rimase pieno di tanta grazia della desiderata virtude della umilta e del lume di Dio, che d'allora innanzi egli era sempre *in giubbilo*: e spesse volte quando egli orava, facea un giubbilo in forma d'uno suono, a modo di Colombo, ottuso, U U I) :e con faccia lieta, e cuore giocondo istava cosi in contemplazione; e con questo, essendo divenuto umilissimo, si riputava minore di tutti gli uomini del mondo. Domandato da Frate Jacopo da Fallerone, perche nel suo giubbilo egli non mutava verso, ripuose con grande letizia; che quando in una cosa si truova ogni bene, non bisogna mutare verso." *Fioretti* cap. 32. Also a good English translation Is Gianluigi Pasquale, Day by Day with St. Francis (Hyde Park, New City Press, 2011) p. 131.

of spiritual melodies would often well up within him and found expression in French melodies, and the murmurs of God's voice, heard by him alone, would joyfully pour forth in French-like jubilations."[109]

Large groups of people could enter into jubilation. One of the more beautiful accounts of this is Thomas of Celano's account of a Christmas Eve celebration in Greccio. Men and women from all over the region came to join the friars to celebrate the wonder of the birth of the Savior. A manger scene with crib was made, and the large crowd jubilated all night. Here is Thomas of Celano's amazing description of this tender and exuberantly joyful celebration of the birth of the Savior: "A manger has been prepared, hay has been brought, and an ox and an ass have been led up to the place... The people arrive, and they are gladdened with wondrous delight at the great mystery. The woods resound with their voices and the rocks re-echo their jubilations. The friars sing and give due praise to the Lord, and all the night rings with jubilation. The saint of God (Francis) stands before the manger, sighing, overwhelmed with devotion and flooded with ecstatic joy. The sacrifice of the Mass is celebrated over the manger, and the priest experiences a new consolation."[110]

AN ACCOUNT OF WONDER AND JOY

Perhaps the most beautiful description of expressive worship

---

109 I have included the Latin. "Ebrius amore et compasione Christi beatus Franciscus quandeque talia faciebat; nam dulcissima melodia spiritus intra ipsum ebulliens frequenter exterius gallicum dabat sonum; et vena divini susurrii quam auris ejus suscipiebat furtive, gallicum erumpebat in jubilum." *Fratre Leone, Speculum Perfectionis, ed. Paul Abatier* (Paris:Librairie Fischabcher, Rue de Seine 33, 1898) cap. 93.

110 I have included the Latin jubilation reference in the Thomas of Celano quote. Ad veniunt populi et ad novum musteria exitit: adveniunt populi, et ad novum mysterium novis gaudis adlaetantur. Personat sylva voces, et jubilantibus rupes respondent. Cantant Fratres, Domino laudes debitas per Salventes. Et tota nox jubilatione resultat. Thomas of Celano, *Vita Prima*, Acta Sanctorum Octobris Tomus Secundus, p. 706.

ever written is the account by Celano of the canonization of Francis. The life of Francis had been like a lyric poem. His love, his strength, and his tenderness had touched tens of thousands before his death. When the announcement came that the Pope was to declare him a saint, people danced in the streets.

The Pope made the trip to Assisi to declare him numbered among the saints. When the Pope, Gregory IX, arrived in Assisi, the city was "filled with gladness," the crowd of people marked the occasion "with great jubilation, and the brightness of the day was made brighter by the torches they brought."[111]

Then Thomas of Celano gives the account of the actual canonization. (This is a first-hand account; he was doubtless present at the canonization.) An account was read of the miracles and life of Francis. The Pope was so moved by this account that he "breathed deep sighs that rose from the bottom of his heart, and, seeking relief in repeated sobs, he shed a torrent of tears. The other prelates of the Church likewise poured forth a flood of tears, so that their sacred vestments were dampened by the abundant flow. Then all the people began to weep."[112]

The Pope lifted up his hands to heaven and proclaimed Francis enrolled among the saints. "At these words the reverend cardinals, together with the Lord Pope, began to sing the *Te Deum* in a loud voice. Then there was raised a clamor among the many people praising God: the earth resounded with their mighty voices, the air was filled with their jubilations, and the ground was moistened with their tears. New songs were sung, and the servants of God jubilated in melody of the Spirit. Sweet sounding organs were heard there and spiritual hymns were sung with well-

---

111 *Early Franciscan Classics*, p. 127.
112 *Early Franciscan Classics*, p. 130.

modulated voices. There a very sweet odor was breathed, and a most joyous melody that stirred the emotions resounded there."[113]

In this account we see amazing similarities to group singing in the Spirit, as practiced in the present day charismatic renewal. It shows that ordinary people during this period could enter into Spirit-led songs in groups. Those familiar with medieval literature know that this was not just an isolated incident. As we shall see, whole cities and towns during times of religious exultation could enter into this type of praise. This, and the other accounts we shall look at, show us that spontaneous Spirit-led worship was still a part of the Church at this late date.

RENEWALS AND REVIVALS

The Age of Faith was a time of many renewals and revivals. Jubilation and exuberant praise could be a vital part of those revivals. Wandering preachers would go through the countryside preaching a turning to God. The results were often that whole towns would lay aside the implements of war and that many would join such orders as the Franciscans and the Dominicans.

We have a remarkable account of one of these revivals that took place in northern Italy in 1233. It was known as the Alleluia. The Franciscan chronicler Sambilene has left us a vivid account of this revival.

The revival included outdoor preaching. The response of the people is astounding, similar to the group praise of the modern day charismatic renewal. Large crowds entered into jubilation and spontaneous song while walking in processions with banners and lighted torches. Sambilene

---

113 Thomas of Celano, *St. Francis of Assisi: First and Second Life of St. Francis* with Selections from the *Treatise on the Miracles of Blessed Francis*, trans. Placid Hermann (Chicago: Franciscan Herald Press, 1963), 69.

describes such scenes:

> This Alleluia, which lasted for a certain length of time, was a period of peace and quiet, in part because the weapons of war had been laid aside. It was a time of merriment and gladness, of joy and exultation, of praise and jubilation. During this time men of all sorts sang songs of praise to God—gentle and simple people, townspeople and farmers, young men and young women. Old people and young people were of one mind. This turning to God was experienced in all the cities of Italy, and they came from the villages to the town with banners, a great multitude of people, men and women, boys and girls together, to hear the preaching and to (gather together) to praise God. The songs that they sang were of God, not of man, and all walked in the way of salvation. And they carried branches of trees and lighted torches. Sermons were preached in the evening, in the morning and at noon... Also, men took their places in churches and outdoors and lifted up their hands to God, to praise and bless him for ever and ever. They (wished) that they would never have to stop from praising God, they were so drunk with his love. How happy was the man that could do the most to praise God.[114]

Both the word jubilation and the allusion to spiritual inebriation are used in this passage. It is nearly certain that in using these terms Sambilene is indicating spontaneous song and jubilation. There are strong similarities in this account and in the account of the canonization of Francis.

Many of the styles of the wandering preachers were amazingly similar to preaching styles among classical Pentecostals. Some of the preachers, like Benedict of Parma, did not belong to orders. Others were Dominicans and Franciscans.

---

114 *Monumenta Germaniae* (vol. XXXII, Scriptores) 70.

John of Parma had an exuberant preaching style, and could lead congregations into that style. He often carried with him a trumpet. Carrying his trumpet he went about "preaching and praising God in the churches and the open places."

Sambilene gives a picturesque description of John's preaching: "I myself have often seen him preaching and praising God. He often did this standing upon the wall of the bishop's palace which was at that time in the process of being built. He began his praises by saying in the vulgar tongue, 'Praised and blessed and glorified be the Father.' Then the children would repeat the same words. A second time he would repeat the phrase, adding 'be the Son,' and the children would repeat the same and sing the same words. For the third time he would repeat the phrase, adding 'be the Holy Ghost,' and then 'Alleluia, alleluia, alleluia!' Afterward he would blow his trumpet. Then he would preach, adding a few words in praise of God."

This account of the Alleluia shows there could be a great deal of spontaneity in the religious life of thirteenth-century Christians. Their spontaneous song, their great love of praising God, and their use of banners and torches remind one of the large processions with banners, candles and inspired songs many at charismatic conferences.

CHARISMATIC PRAYER AND CATHEDRALS

One of the best examples of religious renewals in the Middle Ages was the building of cathedrals. These cathedrals were often built as part of a wave of religious zeal that would sometimes grip whole towns, cities and regions. A good bit of the work was done by volunteers in an atmosphere of group charismatic prayer. It has been noted that if all we knew of the Middle Ages were the churches and the cathedrals passed down to us, we would know practically all we need to know about their faith. Richly carved altars, statues, and windows illuminated with light filtering through stained glass moved men to a deep experience of God.

The queen of cathedrals was Chartres. Its many windows also spoke beautifully of the place of Jesus in redemption. Windows depicting his infancy, his life and his crucifixion give a pictorial glimpse of the deep devotion that people of that time had to a warmly human Jesus.

The first part of the cathedral at Chartres, begun in 1145, was built as a result of a religious revival that swept Normandy. Contemporary accounts describe this revival that began in Chartres and spread to Dives and then throughout Normandy. One letter by a participant in this revival, Abbot Haimon of St. Pierre-sur-Dives in Normandy, vividly describes this revival, and the accuracy of his account is attested by other contemporary sources. Charismatic worship healing services and a greater call to conversion were all a part of this revival. A great amount of the work on the cathedral was done by volunteer labor. The number of volunteer workers seems to have been in the thousands—an astounding figure when it is remembered that the population of Chartres was only ten thousand at this time. The renewal that led to the building of the cathedral was seen as an act of grace on the part of God.

God looked down in his mercy because people had become "estranged from God" and "sick with sin." The renewal came because "the loving Lord looked from heaven...and then he drew to himself those who had moved away from him, and recalled the wandering." In doing so God showed the people at Chartres "a new manner of seeking him."

A strong element in the renewal involved conversion. To join the voluntary association that built the cathedral, Haimon says that men and women had to go to confession, put away grudges and make up with enemies. During the actual building of the cathedral, priests exhorted the crowds to greater conversion of heart.

Both nobility and common serfs worked as equals in doing the manual work so important to the building of the cathedral. Haimon's words leap across the centuries as he describes the spirit of love and conversion that permeated the work on the cathedral:

> For who ever beheld, who ever heard, in all the ages past that kings, princes, the powerful men of this world, proud of their birth and their wealth, used to a life of ease, harness themselves to a wagon and haul a load of stone, lime, wood or some other building material. The load was so heavy that sometimes more than a thousand people were required to pull the wagon... When they stopped to rest nothing was heard but confession of sins and pure prayer to God... The priests encouraged the group to be of one mind; hatreds ceased, grudges disappeared... and men's hearts were united.

Charismatic prayer and prayer for healing played an important part in the renewal. Trumpets and banners accompanied the work of moving stone to the cathedral. Haimon speaks of "blasts of trumpets and waving of banners...too marvelous to tell of." When the priests encouraged the people to repent and seek mercy, they would break into charismatic prayer. They would "lift up their sobs and sighs from the inmost recesses of their hearts with the voice of confession and praise." Many would be so overcome with God's presence that they would "fall to the ground, then lie there with outstretched arms and kiss the earth again and again."

According to Haimon innumerable healings accompanied

the prayer and work: "If I would tell all that I have been allowed to see, even in a single night, my memory and my tongue would utterly fail me."

During the moving of the stone they would stop the wagons and pray for the sick. Then "you may see the dumb open their mouths to praise God. Those troubled by demons come to sounder mind... The sick and those troubled by various diseases get up healed from the wagons on which they have been laid."

Night was a time for rest and spontaneous prayer and healing services. The wagons pulled up around the beginnings of the church. Torches and lights of all sorts were lighted on the wagons. The sick were set apart in groups. The people sang "psalms and hymns" and then implored the Lord and his mother to heal the sick. When all the sick were not healed at first, the crowd would become even more exuberant in its prayer. Cries and tears would be sent up to heaven. People even went to excess and would throw themselves on the ground and crawl toward the high altar. They would be moved to an excess of penance.

After much fervent prayer, a startling scene took place. Haimon continues: "Soon all the sick leap forth healed from wagon after wagon. The crippled throw away the crutches on which they had leaned their crippled limbs, hurrying to give thanks at the altar. Blind men see and move about with ease." After each healing there was a procession to the high altar and bells were rung. Throughout the night "nothing is heard but hymns, praises and thanks!"[115]

The letter we have just examined by Abbot Haimon is a remarkable document. It shows clearly that charismatic

---

115 Haimon's letter can be found in Coulton's Anthology. Most of the account of the wonder of Chartres is drawn from Haimon's letter. I have changed the English to a more readable modern style. Coulton, vol. II. pp. 18-22.

prayer and worship were a part of the renewal that produced what is perhaps the best Christian art and architecture in the history of the Church.

There was a glossolalia element in their prayer. The "sighs" that came from the "inmost recesses of their heart" were given over to praise as Haimon says. Here again we have wordless vocalized prayer to express a deep love of God.

Hymns and praises lasted late into the night. There is also an obvious connection between fervent expressive prayer and healing. There were also obvious excesses at Chartres. The crawling on the ground and times of excessive penance were probably not the best ways to express one's fervor. Still, the faith of the crowd in seeking God for healing and being willing to spontaneously express that prayer with their bodies and voices says much about the place of expressive prayer in the healing ministry and the connection between spontaneity and artistic creativity.

OTHER SOURCES

Examples of jubilation and expressive worship as a seemingly ordinary part of medieval religious expression abound. A look at several examples will give an idea of how widespread this type of spontaneous expression might have been.

LITURGICAL SERVICES

Whole congregations and groupings of people could break out into spontaneous prayer. One example is the joyful occasion of the finding of the body of St. Genevieve after it was thought to have been lost. This happened during the midst of a church service.

William, the canon of the Church, broke out into jubilation and then led the congregation in the *Te Deum*. The author of the account paraphrases St. Gregory's definition of jubilation as a joy beyond words that still must be expressed. The account reads: "He (William) contained no longer the joy which his soul had conceived; but, forgetting those who were of greater authority than himself, he burst forth into sounds of exultation, and boldly raised the *Te Deum*, so that the whole church resounded with the might of his voice; whereupon the whole people, who had come together for this solemn day, took it up with no less alacrity than he, and sang it to the end, after which the archbishop continued with the collect for the saintly virgin's day."[116]

Thomas a Becket

This same type of spontaneous outburst can be seen in the record of events following the martyrdom of St. Thomas a Becket, the archbishop of Canterbury, who was murdered by friends of the king. After his death, as a group of monks prepared his body for burial, they discovered that he was wearing a hair shirt underneath his clothes, a sign that he had been leading a life of prayer and self-denial similar to a monk's. As the realization of his holiness dawned on the monks, they broke into wordless shouts. "Then the monks, wholly transported with spiritual joy, lifted their hearts and hands to heaven, glorifying God; they gave over sorrow for rejoicing, turned their laments to cries of gladness."[117]

Early Cistercian Literature

Examples of this more ordinary type of expressive worship can be found in early Cistercian literature, particularly the biographies of St. Bernard, an active man who preached all over Europe in support of the Crusades and against heresy.

An example can be seen in the effect his preaching had on the emperor of the Holy Roman Empire at the imperial city

---

116 Coulton, vol. IV, pp. 186-189.

117 Richard Winston, *Thomas a Becket*, (London: Constable, 1967) p. 361.

of Spires. The emperor was so touched by the preaching that he reacted in the following way: "I acknowledge," he (the emperor) said, with tears, "that God has given me many graces: and, with the help of the Lord, I will not render myself unworthy of them." And he added, "I am ready to devote my life to the Lord, and to go whithersoever he calls me."[118]

The congregation was deeply touched by the emperor's confession of faith and broke into spontaneous worship:

> The people, deeply moved, and astonished at this extraordinary scene, raised their hands to heaven and filled the basilica with prolonged acclamations; the whole city was in a state of excitement and commotion; and the earth re-echoed, afar off, the people's cries of joy and enthusiasm.[119]

A LONG TRADITION

There are some indications in a sixteenth-century English narrative that jubilation continued as a group experience well into the sixteenth century. The account is a part of a contemporary description of the persecutions of Catholics in England during the early Reformation. It describes a Mass at a Carthusian monastery, during those troubled times, in which the monks were overcome with a heavenly melody:

> At that conventual Mass, when he (the celebrant) had reached the most holy Elevation, a kind of sibilant sound, light to the ear, was perceived by many and heard with their bodily ears. The sound, coming from a little ways outside, worked deeply inside them; it was felt by all and was drawn to the ears of

---

118 M. L'Abbe Ratisbonne, *St. Bernard, The Life and Times* (New York: Sadlier and Co., 1855), p. 383.

119 Ratisbonne, p. 383.

the heart. Our venerable Father Prior was touched by this sweet modulation and sound, and was so involved in the plenty of a divine enlightenment and an abundance of tears that he could go no further with the Mass service for some time. Likewise our whole community stood stupefied, hearing the noise indeed, and feeling its wonderful and fine working in our heart.[120]

This look at various aspects of medieval society, and the period immediately following, shows that glossolalia prayer could still be a part of the ordinary experience of average Christians. Glossolalia prayer, along with inspired song and other forms of expressive worship, seems to have been a typical response to important religious events.

There is real indication, also, that glossolalia prayer was not only a spontaneous response but a form of prayer practiced on a regular basis. Brother Masseo, the Franciscan, practiced this form of prayer whenever he was in contemplation.

A good look at some revivals and the building of the cathedrals shows that jubilation, wordless voiced prayer and prayer meetings were a vital part of medieval Catholicism. In the remarkable material on the building of Chartres we find that numerous healings came through the expressive prayers of ordinary Christians.

This look at medieval Catholicism says much to the modern-day charismatic renewal. It shows how integrated miracles and expressive worship were with the whole of life. One senses an un-self-conscious freedom of expression that burst

---

120 Thanks to Phillip O'Meara for the translation of this quote. Dom Maurice Chauncy, Carthusian of London and later of Newport, *Historia aliquit martyrum anglorum* (Historyof certain English martyrs) written in the mid-16th century,published 1888, p. 96: Quoted from R. W. Chambers, *On the Continuity of English Prose From Alfred to More and His School* (London: EETS, Oxford U. Press, 1932, p. CXL. Chapter 5.

out not only in the building of cathedrals but in expressive prayer. There is also an indication of a close connection between the ability of men and women to spontaneously be united in expressive prayer and great works of art, with conversion and renewal taking place.

CHAPTER 6

Mystics—
Singers of a New Song

God makes his friends to be happily foolish.
—Jan Ruysbroeck

Many of us have misconceptions about mystics and mystical prayer. Mystics are often thought of as lonely, solitary men and women who have extraordinary experiences—men and women who are given over to quiet and silence. While there are some mystics who fit these categories, most do not. A good look at original sources finds them deeply involved in intimate human contact. More often than not they possessed an extraordinary sense of humor, and some like St. John Bosco, St. Philip Neri and St. Francis of Assisi elevated buffoonery to a prayer form.

Mystics and mysticism were once a vital part of the life of the Church. Their hunger for God and their evident freedom, tenderness and joy were startling signs of God's Kingdom being lived out among his people. Mystics were persons who deeply centered their lives on the heart of God. They were in the process of astounding transformation. The leaven gave their lives great joy and hope, and a sense of purpose to the whole Christian Church.

Mystics—Singers of a New Song

Their growth toward union with God and with their fellow man was marked by excruciating cleansing and purging as well as times of incomparable wonder.

Mystical Jubilation

Jubilation, which, as we have seen, could be the prayer of ordinary Christians in the Age of Faith, was even more a part of the prayer of mystics in that period and in the following centuries. The terms jubilation and spiritual inebriation refer to the whole gamut of spontaneous bodily and vocal prayer. The term referred to glossolalia prayer, inspired songs, dancing, and strong movements of the body. This form or state of prayer is mentioned by most of the major spiritual writers until the seventeenth century and was experienced by most of the major mystics.

We are lucky to have the works of several nineteenth and early twentieth century scholars on mysticism which give us an overview of the part mystical jubilation played in the lives of mystics. Albert Farges gives this description of mystical jubilation:

> There are even more violent transports, such as those so often observed in St. Francis of Assisi, St. Philip Neri, St. Joseph of Cupertino, St. Mary Magdalene de Pazzi, and many other holy mystics, whose jubilation or spiritual inebriation showed itself outwardly in actions which astonished and even scandalized the weak and ignorant. Such were their sighs, cries, ardent and broken exclamations, abundant tears, and even laughter, songs, improvised hymns, tremors agitating every limb, leapings, impetuous movements, the violent outward

expression of enthusiasm and love.[121]

One of the more thorough studies made on the subject in recent times has been done by John Joseph Gorres in *Die christliche Mystik*. Written in the early nineteenth century, the book had a strong apologetic aim. Its purpose was to defend the Catholic faith and Catholic mysticism against rationalism. A part of his defense of the Catholic faith was to explain and describe a number of mystical phenomena. He did a remarkable job of compiling a number of examples of mystical phenomena from a number of sources.

He has done an extraordinary job of describing and attempting to explain mystical jubilation. He devotes a lengthy chapter to jubilation called "The Effect of Ecstasy on the Organs of the Voice." In this chapter he describes the effects of spiritual experience on the voice. Spiritual experience affects the voice by enabling it to sing heavenly melodies in one's own language, or a language unknown to the person praying. The same process produces prophetic words, etc.

This process begins with the normal human process of speech. These normal human speech organs are changed during spiritual experience. He says: "The forces which contribute to the formation of this sound (ordinary speech) can also submit to a transformation in ecstasy and the sounds produced in this state carry a character which is much different from ordinary sounds." One is brought to a point where "the spirit self is articulated in these sounds, words which the spirit of man hadn't thought. The voice then produces sounds which seem to belong to someone else. Or if this is really the voice of one speaking, it is like elevated or winged thoughts which are spoken."[122]

---

121 Albert Farges, *Mystical Phenomena* (New York:Benziger Brothers, 1926) p. 155.

122 John Joseph Gorres, *La Mystique* (French version of *Die Christiliche Mystik*, Paris: Mme Vve Poussielgue- Rusand, Libraire, 1854) vol 2, p. 149.

The effect of spiritual experience on the voice could cause one to be able to speak a language that one had never learned. Gorres gives the example of St. Mary Magdalene de Pazzi who was able to speak Latin, a language she had never learned.[123] Predictive prophecy was another effect of religious experience on the voice according to Gorres.[124]

Gorres gives a number of examples of inspired song. One of his more vivid descriptions is St. Humiliane. The sisters in her convent would hear glossolalia—like songs coming from her, "a beautiful song with a voice so delicate that when they didn't have their ears right up to her mouth, they heard the song but were unable to distinguish words."[125]

Gorres gives descriptions of expressive movement accompanied by glossolalia song. In ecstasy, Christine the Admirable would "turn around like a doll agitated by several children." Then there would come from her "a marvelous song which nobody was able to understand or imitate in spite of all efforts. There was in this song a very fluid element...and the succession of these sounds. But the words of these melodies, if one wants to call them words, were sometimes incomprehensible." [126] After her spiritual song Christine was overcome by spiritual drunkenness. Gorres' account reads: "Little by little she appeared to be drunk—she was drunk in effect, but with a holy and divine drunkenness." She led the other sisters in the singing of the *Te Deum*.[127]

The beauty of this jubilation of Christine was angelic.

---

[123] Gorres, p. 150.

[124] The ecstatic predictions of Jeanne de la Croix are cited as an example of the prophetic gift resulting from the giving over of the voice in ecstasy. Gorres, p. 155.

[125] Gorres, p. 158.

[126] Gorres, p. 159.

[127] Gorres, p. 159.

Gorres says that her song was so beautiful when she sang in this manner that "it seemed to be the voice of an angel rather than the song of a mortal. It was so beautiful to hear that it surpassed not only the sounds of the most beautiful instruments but even the most pleasant human voice."[128]

She was also able to sing in Latin, a language she did not know and had never learned.[129] Here we see a real connection between the spontaneous song of jubilation and the speaking of a language one has never learned.

Gorres gives many similar accounts from the lives of other holy people. Invisible choirs were heard singing around certain holy people.[130]

It is clear that this jubilation could clearly be inarticulate glossolalia prayer. Gorres says of Christine: "This was the jubilation of her soul which came out in unarticulated sounds."[131] Gorres thus sees prophecy, the ability to sing or speak in a language one has never learned and glossolalia prayer as part of the experience of giving one's voice over to spiritual experience—the giving over of the natural human organ of the voice to the move of the Spirit.

There are remarkable similarities in Gorres' presentation of these phenomena and the way that they are experienced in

---

128 Gorres, p. 159.

129 Gorres, p. 159.

130 "There were other sounds which were heard around them (saints) which could not be traced to their origin, and which one could only attribute to some sort of superior beings...Often during the divine service—especially Mass—one often heard invisible choirs making sounds around one of the holy people singing the sanctus or some other chants. The examples are so frequent...We will be content to cite examples just from the Order of Friars Minor. Among those favored with this gift were: Antoine de Ganazas, Lucius Dominique, Marie d'Amarante, Cath Bernardine, Helene Riderin, Jeanne de Saint-Etienne, Marie Suarez, Marie de Lucie, Bernardin de Rhegio, Ann Daberhoferin, Cunegonde de Sandacio, Leonore Ulloa, Cath. Menriquia." Gorres, p. 160.

131 Gorres, p. 14.

charismatic renewal. In both, spontaneous song, glossolalia prayer, speaking a language one has never learned, and prophecy are seen as aspects of the same basic spiritual operation.

JUBILATION: AN ENTRANCE INTO THE DEEPER SPIRITUAL LIFE

The gift of tongues is often looked upon in charismatic renewal as an entrance to a deeper spiritual life. The same appears to be true in the spiritual experience of the mystics. Evelyn Underhill makes this point in her biography of Jacopone da Todi. She calls jubilation "the characteristic phenomena of the beginner in the supersensual life,"[132] and she adds: "These acute emotional reactions, often accompanied by eccentric outward behavior, are a normal episode in the early development of many mystics, upon whom the beauty and wonder of the new world of spirit now perceived by them, and the Presence that fills it, have often an almost intoxicating effect."[133]

This suggestion of Underhill is borne out in the writings of many of the mystics. As Ruysbroeck calls jubilation the "first and lowest mode whereby God inwardly declares himself in the contemplative life."[134]

Richard Rolle received the gift of heavenly song early in the development of his spiritual life as a definite experience. Gordic received this as a definite experience also. On a pilgrimage to the Holy Land he spent whole nights praying on the mountains and visiting the Holy Sepulcher with unspeakable devotion. Afterward he had a definite experience of jubilation. His biographer describes it: "In

---

132 Underhill, *Jacopone*, p. 76.

133 Ibid, 78.

134 John Ruysbroeck, *The Book of the Twelve Bequines*, ch. X. As quoted in Underhill, *Jacopone*, 78.

his heart there was a gentleness greater than anything else, in his mouth a sweetness sweeter than honey on the honeycomb, and his ears were filled with the melody of a great jubilation."[135]

We see then, that for many contemplatives, entering into the wonder of God with one's voice and body was a natural part of entering into a deeper spiritual life. There is a strong similarity between this form of initiation and tongues as a form of initiation among charismatics in the present-day charismatic renewal.

Jacopone Da Todi

One of the more exciting mystics in the history of the Church was Jacopone da Todi (1228-1306), the Franciscan friar who wrote the famous hymn *Stabat Mater*. Jubilation was one of the central points in his spirituality.

Before his conversion he enjoyed a happy life as a jurist. He was deeply in love with his pretty young wife. One day while he and his wife were attending a wedding celebration, in the midst of a dance, the floor fell with a crash and his wife lay dead. When her party dress was removed a hair shirt was found on her body, a sign that she was a woman of prayer who had been praying for the conversion of her husband. Jacopone, profoundly shaken by this, sold all his possessions and eventually joined the Franciscans.[136] After many years of purging he entered into a period of overflowing spiritual joy. He describes his mystic journey in a number of songs and poems.

One whole period of his development recorded in his songs and poetry deals with jubilation. We are lucky to have

---

135 Eric Colledge, *The Medieval Mystics of England* (New York: Charles Scribner's Sons, 1961), p. 39.

136 Karl Vossier, *Medieval Culture* (New York: Frederick Ungar Pub. Co., 1929), vol. II, pp. 83-84.

Evelyn Underhill's masterful study of Jacopone's jubilation period in her biography. During this period, Underhill says that he "babbled of love with 'tears and laughter, sorrow and delight,' and with gestures that seemed foolishness to other men."[137]

He describes this state of jubilation in his poems. In "La Bontade se lamenta" he paints a vivid picture of the state of a soul in jubilation. In this poem he calls this state a "new language." His words tremble with excitement: Now a new language doth she speak, "Love, Love," is all her tongue can say, She weeps, and laughs; rejoices, mourns, In spite of fears, is safe and gay; And though her wits seem all astray,— So wild, so strange, her outward mien—Her soul within her is serene; And heeds not how her acts appear.[138]

Again in another poem he describes this jubilation as a joy of abundance that breaks forth in the voice: Abundance cannot hide herself apart; And jubilation, from out her nest within the heart, Breaks forth in song, and in sibilant sound (sibilare) Even as did Elias long ago.[139] Jacopone penetrated into the hilarity and love at the heart of God:

> "For since God's wisdom, though so great, Is all intoxicate, with love, Shall mine not be inebriate? And so be like my Lord above? No greater honour can I prove Than sharing His insanity."[140]

In his poem "Of the Jubilus of the Heart, That Breaks Forth in the Voice" Jacopone personifies and addresses the jubilus as though it were a person. Again this points out what a real and personal concept the jubilus was to him.

---

137 Underhill, *Jacopone*, p. 76.

138 Underhill, *Jacopone*, p. 76.

139 Underhill, *Jacopone*, p. 77.

140 Underhill, *Jacopone*, p. 79.

This poem is the most significant poem of his jubilation period. In it he describes jubilation as a "childish stammering" in which one does not know what one is saying. It is so expressive that those uninitiated into the mystical life think the speaker foolish and stand apart.

This jubilation of Jacopone indicates that the heart is going through the deep purification of an intense love relationship with God and shows that the heart is "deep-pierced" by God's love:

Of the Jubilus of the Heart That Breaks Forth in the Voice
Thou, Jubilus, the heart dost move;

And makst us sing for very love. The Jubilus in fire awakes, And straight the man must sing and pray, His tongue in *childish stammering shakes, Nor knows he what his lips may say*; He cannot quench nor hide away That Sweetness pure and infinite. The Jubilus in flame is lit, And straight the man must shout and sing; So close to Love his heart is knit, He scarce can bear the honeyed sting; His clamour and cries must ring, And shame forever take to flight. The Jubilus enslaves man's heart —A love-bewildered prisoner—And see! his neighbours stand apart, And mock the *senseless chatterer*, They deem his speech a foolish blur, A shadow of his spirit's light. Yea, when thou enterest the mind, O Jubilus, thou rapture fair, The heart of man new skill doth find Love's own disguise to grasp and wear, The suffering of Love to bear, With song and clamour of delight! And thus the uninitiate will deem that thou art crazed indeed; They see thy strange and fervered state, But have not wit thy heart to read; Within, deep-pierced, that heart may bleed, Hidden from curious mortal sight.[141]

---

141 Underhill, *Jacopone*, pp. 279-281.

More Mystics

We find many instances of jubilation used in personal prayer, and in Church too. One modern schoar of mysticism in the twelfth century, Paul Mommaers writes of of Richard of St. Victor, a spiritual writer from that period.

Richard of St. Victor(1173 ACE)

A medieval scholar of spiritual experience distinguishes between the jubilus of the heart and that of the lips, but in both cases it is one and the same emotion which has a manifold effect: "In the jubilus of the heart it is one sweetness that is poured out over us but the joy is manifold; in the jubilus of the the lips the dance (of the melody) around one and the same syllable multiplies itself..."[142]

Richard characterizes the phenomenon thus:

> "And in the meeting with the light, pleasure and delight are so great that the heart cannot bear it, but bursts forth for joy through the voice: and this is called jubilation or jubilation, that is, a joy which cannot be expressed in words." (Page 29)

> We find jubilation still continuing in full force during the thirteenth century. Thomas of Cantimpre reports Christina of Sint-Truiden, who died c. 1224 while sitting in her Church would be "gripped by the jubilus which would 'resound in an unforgettable way' from her throat and chest." (Page 28)

Petrus Dacus records that during his second visit to Christine of Stommelen in 1268:

> "She started to speak. And with that she burst out in jubilation as a joyous excitement ran through her

---

[142] Paul Mommaers, *Hadewijch: Writer, Beguine, Love Mystic* (Leuren: Peeters, DL, 2004).

entire body, which looked like a very unusual sort of rocking movement. The jubilation took one breath which lasted one whole miserere and was then followed by motionlessness which lasted the same length of time." (Page 29)

Ruysbroek sounds a word of caution, "One should be prepared to abandon such a jubilus every now and then for something better and on occasion do a work of charity..." (Page 29)

John Ruysbroeck and Henry Suso

The Black Death, the rise of nationalism and other factors began the unwinding of the medieval spiritual synthesis. Spirituality lost much of its un-self-conscious innocence. Spiritual writers became more and more introspective and speculative. Even though much of the simplicity and naivete was lost, this move meant that the experience of transforming union with God was explored in much greater detail.

The fourteenth century, the time of the beginning of this unwinding, was also a time when mysticism flourished. Perhaps the most significant school of mysticism during the fourteenth century was the Rhineland School, a tradition of mystics in the low countries of Europe. The best known and most revered men in this tradition of mysticism were Blessed John Ruysbroeck and Blessed Henry Suso.

John Ruysbroeck. Ruysbroeck mentions jubilation a number of times in his writings. For him it meant the whole of bodily and vocal spontaneous expression of spiritual movement within a soul. It could be quite exuberant, making some of the expressive worship of modern-day pentecostals seem tame in comparison. He says:

Spiritual inebriation is this: That a man receives

> more sensible joy and sweetness than his heart can either contain or desire. Spiritual inebriation brings forth many strange gestures in men. It makes some sing and praise God because of their fullness of joy, and some weep with great tears because of their sweetness of heart. It makes one restless in all his limbs, so that he must run and jump and dance; and so excites another that he must gesticulate and clap his hands...
>
> Other things sometimes happen to those who live in the fierce ardour of love; for often another light shines into them...and in the meeting with that light, the joy and the satisfaction are so great, that the heart cannot bear them, but breaks out with a loud voice in cries of joy. And this is called the *jubilus* or jubilation, that is, a joy which cannot be uttered in words.[143]

It is noted that he repeats the classic definition of the *jubilus*, that it is "a joy which cannot be uttered in words." This jubilation is a means by which God makes his friends "happily foolish."[144] Spiritual experience seizes the believer with such power that:

> ...he scarcely knows how to contain himself, and knows not how he should bear himself. For he thinks that no one has ever experienced the things which he is experiencing and from thence arise jubilee (jubilation) because he cannot restrain himself... Such an impatience possesses him outwardly and inwardly with so great a vehemence, that in all his powers and members there is so joyous an

---

143 John Ruysbroeck, *The Adornement of the Spiritual Marriage*, Bk. II., chs xix. and xxiv, as quoted in Underhill, *Jacopone*, p. 78.

144 John Ruysbroeck, *The Adornement of the Spiritual Marriage*, Bk. II., chs xix. and xxiv, as quoted in Underhill, *Jacopone*, p. 78.

experience... God makes his friends to be happily foolish. Sometimes this ecstasy is wont to grow to so great a height that the matter becomes serious, and more frequently he is compelled to break out into shouting whilst he is being spiritually touched or pricked.[145]

For Ruysbroeck, jubilation was a part of a deeply personal relationship with God. The Spirit of the Lord says to the heart: "I am yours, O man, and you are mine: I live in you and you live in me." This touch of God causes "great joy and pure pleasure to occupy body and soul," and the joy is so great that the person cannot endure it. This joy coming from such a personal interaction with God "is called the *jubilus*, which no one can express in words."

This jubilation is praise and thanksgiving. Says Ruysbroeck: "Hence arises the jubilation, which is the love of the heart, and the burning flame of devotion with praise and thanksgiving and constant reverence and veneration toward God."[146]

Again in *Contemplations Opus Praeclarum*, he describes jubilation as part of the giving and receiving from the Lord, part of a mutual touch. "This same mutual touch, whether so in turn to touch and be touched, effects the *jubilus*." In this state of jubilation the "free and generous emotion pours back everything unto God."[147]

Henry Suso

Blessed Henry Suso (1300-1366) also gives examples of the same spiritual operation. For him these experiences

---

145 John Ruysbroeck, *The Kingdom of the Lovers of God*, trans. T. Arnold Hyde (E. P. Dutton and Co., 1919), p. 89.

146 John Ruysbroeck, *On the First Method of True Contemplation, Opera Omnia Ioannis Rusbrochii*, p. 436.

147 John Ruysbroeck, *Contemplatione Opus Preaclarum, Opera Omnia*, p. 469.

also came at points of tender conversations with his Lord: "I had certain tender conversations with my Creator in which only my spirit talked. I wept and sighed; I laughed and cried."[148] In his autobiography, Blessed Henry gives a stirring account of his experiencing inspired songs: One day...while the Servant (Blessed Henry's word for himself) was still at rest he heard within himself a gracious melody by which his heart was greatly moved. And at the moment of the rising of the morning star, a deep sweet voice sang these words, *Stella Maria Maris*... And this song which he heard was so spiritual that his soul was transported by it and he too began to sing joyously... And one day—it was in carnival time—the Servant had continued his prayers until the moment when the bugle of the watch announced the dawn.

And while his senses were at rest, behold! angelic spirits began to sing the fair response... And this song was echoed with a marvelous sweetness in the depths of his soul. And when the angels had sung for some time his soul overflowed with joy; and his feeble body being unable to support such happiness, burning tears escaped from his eyes.[149]

Richard Rolle

Probably no one person has probed the richness of jubilation, of the gift of heavenly song, more than Richard Rolle of Hampole. Rolle (1300-1349) was an English mystic and writer whose work left a strong mark on English literature. Though he is little known in the twentieth century, his mystical works have a richness that can be compared with the richness of St. Bernard or St. Teresa.

---

148 John G. Arintero, *The Mystical Evolution in the Developmentand Vitality of the Church* (St. Louis: B. Herder Book Co., 1951), vol. II, p. 276.

149 Evelyn Underhill, *Mysticism* (England: Methuen and Co. Ltd., 1911, reprinted in 1962, Gresham Press), p. 277.

Rolle was an educated man who studied at the University of Oxford and the Sorbonne in Paris. At both of these places he was doubtlessly exposed to the wealth of literature coming out of many mystical traditions. At the age of eighteen, after he had finished his work at Oxford and before he began his studies at the Sorbonne, he became a hermit. Our modern conception of a hermit is that of a person almost completely cut off from people and who devotes himself to constant prayer and meditation. On the contrary, many hermits of the late Middle Ages received hundreds of visitors, and their hermitages were often near heavily traveled roads. At times they would go out and engage in such activities as preaching. It is true that they both had and needed long periods of solitude, but there was often room for laughter and people in their lives. So it was with Rolle. Thousands of people visited him at his hermitage because of his sanctity and wisdom.[150] He enjoyed "laughing and playing,"[151] as he puts it, with a variety of people, and he was open to work and converse with women as well as with men.[152]

His mystical writings have much of the warmth and tenderness that one finds in the writings of St. Bernard and the writings of the early Franciscans. Jubilation was perhaps the central concept and metaphor in his understanding of mystical experience.

He used the word jubilation hundreds of times in his writings—one hundred and twenty-four times in the *Melody of Love (Melos Amoris)* alone. He also uses such words as "song," "chant" and "melody" as nearly equivalent to jubilation.

---

[150] Heseltine, Introduction, viii.

[151] Frances M. Comper, *The Life and Lyrics of Richard Rolle* (New York: E.P. Dutton and Co. Inc., 1933), p. 178.

[152] Comper, p. 179.

He Heard a Heavenly Melody

The gift of jubilation, or heavenly song, was a definite event in the life of Richard Rolle, an event that marked an entrance to a deeper spiritual life. It occurred four years after his conversion. He was sitting in a chapel one day when he heard a heavenly melody. The melody descended into his heart and he began to sing and give forth the same sound. Here is his description of the experience: "Whilst I sat in the same chapel in the night, before supper, I sang psalms, as I might, and I heard above me the noise as it were of readers or rather singers. Whilst I took heed, praying to heaven with all desire, in what manner I know not, suddenly I received a most pleasant heavenly melody dwelling within my mind. Indeed, my thought was continuously changed into mirth of song, and I had, as it were, praises in my meditation, and in saying prayers and psalms I gave forth the same sound."[153]

Over and over again in his works, he mentions jubilation. It appears that Rolle knew the tradition of the Church on jubilation. He uses the phrase from the psalms: "*Beatus vir qui scit jubilationem,*" a phrase often used as a take-off point for discussing jubilation in the tradition. He says: "To me it seems indeed that contemplation is the joyful song of the love of God taken into the mind, with the sweetness of angelic praise. This is the joy which is the end of perfect prayer, of honest devotion in this life. This is the mirth to be had in the mind for the everlasting lover, breaking out with a great voice into spiritual songs. This is the final and most perfect of all deeds in this life. The psalmist, therefore, says 'Beatus vir qui scit jubilationem,' that is to say, 'Blessed is the man who knows jubilation,' in the contemplation of God."[154]

---

153 Heseltine, introduction, xvi-xvii.

154 Heseltine, 144.

He also used the term spiritual inebriation as an equivalent for jubilation or song, as we have seen other mystical writers in the tradition do. He speaks of this song as a drunkenness: "A man is carried above himself, 'panting with desire only for the Creator.' ...Lifted up to the melody of song, he is inebriated with divine pleasure."[155]

It seems clear that this harmony could be spoken by the voice. For him it was a special uniting of body and soul. He says: "Then I may say that contemplation is a wonderful joy of God's love, which joy is the praise of God that may not be told. That wonderful praise is in the soul, and for abundance of joy and sweetness it ascends into the mouth so that the heart and the tongue accord as one, and body and soul rejoice, living in God."[156]

He describes this same experience in *Contra Amores Mundi*. First the divine song descends into the spirit of man; from there it ascends to his mouth. Rolle says: "Wherefore, too, one who has been made a contemplative man...is perpetually raised to such great joy that he is even permitted to hear the song of the angels. Hence he sings his prayers to God, in a wonderful and indescribable way, because, just as now the heavenly sound descends his spirit, so also, ascending in a superabundance of joy to his own mouth, the same sound is heard." [157]

It appears that Rolle's songs could also be in an intelligible language. Scholars on Rolle suggest that he sang songs about

---

155 Richard Rolle, *Contra Amores Mundi*, edited with introduction of Latin text and a translation by Paul Theiner (Berkeley: University of California Press, 1968), p. 26.

156 Heseltine, p. 50.

157 Rolle, *Contra Amores*, Theiner, pp. 160-161.

Jesus and Mary spontaneously out of his gift of song.[158]

This is suggested in the *Amending of Life*, where he mentions his prayer being turned into song: "Our heart being kindled with a fervent love, our prayer also is kindled and offered from our mouth in the savour of sweetness in the sight of God, so that it is a great joy to pray. For whilst in prayer a marvelous sweetness is given to him who prays, the prayer is changed into song."[159]

Heseltine strongly suggests that the many poems and songs composed by Rolle were inspired songs: "His verse is the rushing forth of the melody that is within him, a melody of inspiration, however feebly the expression of it may read... He bursts into lyric verse as the spirit moves him."[160]

As we have seen in the chapter on the Age of Faith, Rolle had a great love for the personal Jesus. The word "Jesus" is constantly on his lips. Repetition of the name of Jesus was an important form of prayer for him. The phrase "jubilation in Jesus" is one he uses frequently.[161]

Whenever he prays he uses the name of Jesus: "I cannot pray, I cannot meditate, but in sounding the name of Jesus."[162] And the name of Jesus leads to song: "The name of Jesus has taught me to sing."[163] For Rolle there is a jubilation, a

---

158 "This divine melody chiming from above and resounding in his breast which henceforth is full of delightful harmony, so that his thought, his very prayers, turn into songs to Jesus or Mary, and that he now modulates what before he used to say—what can it mean but the awakening of his poetical powers, which to him appear a miraculous gift imparted at the height of the ecstasies?" C. Horstman, *Richard Rolle of Hampole: An English Father of the Church and His Followers* (London: Swan Sonnenchein and Co., 1895), vol. II, p. vii (note 2).

159 Heseltine, 130.

160 Heseltine, p. xxviii.

161 Rolle, *Chant D'Amour*, vol. II. p. 286.

162 Heseltine, 81.

163 Heseltine, 82.

song at the heart of God. God himself is "a melody sweet as honey, a comforting song and a joyful jubilation."[164]

Jesus is the melody, the jubilation. Rolle says in an inspired song: "Jesus, my Dear and my Darling! My delight is to sing to thee! Jesus, my Mirth and my Melody!"[165]

The fourteenth century mystic, Richard Rolle, calls jubilation of cantor or song. He writes in the Fire of Love:

> Because he has continually given himself to constant devotion for God when Christ wills he shall receive,... a Holy sound sent from heaven, and thought and meditation shall be changed into song, and the mind shall bide in marvelous melody... smoothly it happens to such a lover what I have not found in the writing of the Doctors; that is, this song shall swell up in his mouth...[166]

In Rolle we see many parallels with the modern charismatic renewal. He had a constant tender devotion to the name of Jesus which he used frequently in his prayers. Like modern charismatics, the gift of heavenly song played an important part in his prayer life. He was also in the habit of singing his prayers aloud in English or Latin with inspired melodies.

However, while there are similarities, there are also differences. Rolle's experience of the gift of song seems to be a deeper experience than the gift of tongues. This song allowed him to penetrate heaven, to more fully enter the heart of God. Much of the wondrous part of God, the indescribable part of God, is known in the rhythms and movement of music and sound. Jubilation, the gift of song, was a way of knowing that deep part of God.

---

164 Rolle, *Chant D'Amour*, Ch. 46, 141.
165 Heseltine, 95.
166 As found in Chambers, p. 29.

St. Teresa and St. John

In the sixteenth century, mysticism took a bright new turn in the lives and writings of St. Teresa of Avila and St. John of the Cross. Close friends, these Spanish mystics explored with both heart and intellect the experience of union with God.

Influences. Teresa and John did not develop their mysticism in a vacuum. They were both well-educated and acutely aware of the mystical writings that had come before them. They were aware of many of the medieval concepts of mysticism and familiar with many of the major writers.

One influence on them was Luis of Granada, a Spanish spiritual writer in the early sixteenth century. He was one of St. Teresa's Dominican confessors as well as a popular preacher. His aim was to formulate a spirituality for people living in the world.

In his teaching Luis always strove to be practical. At the same time he was a scholar aware of what had come before him in the mystical tradition. In his *Guide for Preachers*, he repeats, in the sixteenth century, the tradition on jubilation.

He quotes Gregory the Great's classic definition that jubilation "is a joy of the inner man so great that it cannot be expressed in words but is expressed in exterior actions."[167] This jubilation is so great that "neither Plato, the prince of the philosophers, nor Demosthenes, the greatest of orators, were lifted up to this good thing." For Fr. Luis, God was the giver of the gift of jubilation: "God is the author and principle of this joy that we call jubilation."[168]

---

167 Louis De Granada, *Oeuvres Completes*, (Paris: Libraire De Louis Vives, Editeur, 1894) vol. X, 199.

168 Heseltine, 81.

Teresa

St. Teresa is one of the most widely read writers on prayer in the mystical tradition. Though she explored the heights of union with God she was startingly human. A naturalness, a candor and a human warmth pervade her works.

Dance, inspired song and group jubilation were a part of the worship of the reformed Carmelite Order which she founded and headed. Teresa was happy and gay and wanted everyone around her to be happy and cheerful. She didn't want dour-faced nuns, "I won't have nuns who are ninnies," she said. She let her nuns know that "gloomy saints" were not to her liking.

It is said that her laughter was so infectious that when she laughed, the whole convent laughed with her.[169] She and her nuns had a warm sense of community and would frequently enter into exuberant praise and worship. Maurice Auclair in his biography of Teresa brings together original source material on the expressive worship of Teresa and her nuns:

> While they got on with their spinning, they chatted and composed *coplas* (little songs) which the young ones sang very charmingly. Teresa improvised poems which her nuns memorized... One can feel the rhythm of the music.[170]

Dance also played a significant part in the prayer of Teresa and her nuns. Says Auclair:

> For Teresa of Jesus, tenderness and gaiety were such innocent manifestations of the love of one's neighbor and thus of the love of God that even at recreation, fervour took possession of her and she

---

169 Marcelle Auclair, *St. Teresa of Avila* (New York: Pantheon Books, 1953) p. 220.
170 Auclair, p. 220.

became incapable of resisting the urge of the spirit. She would begin to dance, turning round and round and clapping her hands as King David danced before the ark; the nuns accompanied her "in a perfect transport of spiritual joy."[171]

Later when some of her nuns went to France to found Carmelite convents there, the French nuns, to their great surprise, saw the mother superior "more like a seraphim than a mortal creature executing a sacred dance in the choir, singing and clapping her hands in the Spanish way, but with so much dignity, sweetness and grace, that, filled with holy reverence, they felt themselves wholly moved by divine grace and their hearts raised to God."[172]

It is interesting to note that the dancing was, at times, done "in choir," that is, in the context of the divine office, thus having a liturgical setting. Teresa and her nuns could be overwhelmed by the spiritual power of improvised singing. One Easter, Teresa asked one of the nuns to sing an improvised song. She sang:

> May my eyes behold thee, Good and sweet Jesus...
> Let him who will, delight his gaze With jasmine and with roses. If I were to see thee, A thousand gardens would lie before my eyes.[173]

Teresa was so overwhelmed with this song that she fell unconscious in ecstasy. When she came to, she herself sang an improvised song. From then on when she would go into ecstasy, her nuns would surround her and sing softly.[174]

So we see in Teresa and her nuns not only refreshing

---

171 Auclair, p. 221.

172 Auclair, p. 222.

173 Auclair, p. 222.

174 Auclair, p. 223.

examples of expressive worship, but group sharing, in prayer and mystical experience. The expressive and spontaneous prayer experiences Teresa and her nuns had as a group show us that even at this late date mysticism could still be tied to warm group prayer experiences.

We find several significant references in Teresa's writings to jubilation. She devotes several pages to it in her mystical treatise *Interior Castle*. Using both the terms jubilation and spiritual inebriation to describe her experiences. She says:

> Our Lord sometimes bestows upon the soul a jubilation and a strange kind of prayer, the nature of which it cannot ascertain. I set this down here, so that, if he grants you this favour, you may give him hearty praise and know that such a thing really happens.[175]

When this state of prayer comes upon the soul, the soul wants to share this with everyone. "The joy of the soul is so exceedingly great that it would like not to rejoice in God in solitude, but to tell its joy to all, so that they may help it to praise our Lord."

In this state the soul wants to make great festivities like those made for the prodigal son when he returned to his father. The soul wants all to join in her delight: "She would like to invite everybody and have great festivities." The soul in this state "cannot be expected to keep silence and dissemble." The soul must speak forth its praises like St. Francis "going about the countryside crying aloud…that he was the herald of the great king."[176]

Teresa then uses a metaphor often used with jubilation: "divine madness." She says: "Oh, what a blessed madness,

---

175 St. Teresa of Avila, *Interior Castle*, translated and edited by E. Allison Peers (New York: Doubleday, 1961), p. 167.

176 Teresa, *Interior Castle*, p. 168.

sisters! If only God would give it to us all!"[177]

Part of the grace of this style of prayer is to show others the goodness of God. She continues: "And how good he has been to you in placing you here; if the Lord should grant you this grace and you show others that he has done so, you will not be spoken against as you would be in the world (where there are so few to proclaim God's praise that it is not surprising if they are spoken against) but will be encouraged to praise him the more."[178]

> This jubilation could be a group experience. This group experience of jubilation is probably something like the scenes of spontaneous dancing and improvised singing to which we have already referred. She de scribes sisters inspiring one another to praise God. She says: "Sometimes he makes me especially glad when we are together and I see these sisters of mine so full of inward joy that each vies with the rest in praising our Lord for bringing her to the convent; it is very evident that those praises come from the inmost depths of the soul. I should like you to praise him often, sisters, for, when one of you begins to do so, she arouses the rest. How can your tongues be better employed, when you are together, than in the praises of God, which we have so many reasons for rendering him?"[179]

She then goes on to describe jubilation as a prayer that is supernatural and may last all day, and as a form of spiritual inebriation:

> "May it please his majesty often to bestow this prayer upon us since it brings us such security and

---

[177] Teresa, *Interior Castle*, p. 168.

[178] Teresa, *Interior Castle*, p. 168.

[179] Teresa of Avila – *The Complete Works of Teresa of Avila* v12 (e) Volume 2, p. 302.

such benefit. For as it is an entire supernatural thing, we cannot acquire it. It may last for a whole day, and the soul will then be like one who has drunk a great deal..."[180]

She also refers to this style of prayer in her autobiography, using the metaphor of spiritual inebriation to describe this state of prayer. During this state of prayer the soul "knows not whether to speak or be silent, whether to laugh or to weep. This state is a glorious folly, a heavenly madness, in which true wisdom is acquired, and a mode of fruition in which the soul finds the greatest of delight."[181] During this state of jubilation, of spiritual inebriation, the person does many foolish things: "I often used to commit follies because of this love, and to be inebriated with it, yet I had never been able to understand its nature."[182]

The spiritual inebriation of Teresa seems to have a glossolalia aspect. She says: "Many words are spoken, during this state, in praise of God, but, unless the Lord himself puts order into them, they have no orderly form. The understanding, at any rate, counts for nothing here; the soul would like to shout praises aloud, for it is in such a state that it cannot contain itself—a state of delectable disquiet...O God, what must that soul be like when it is in this state! It would fain be all tongue, so that it might praise the Lord. It utters a thousand holy follies, striving ever to please him who thus possesses it."[183]

In Teresa we see a strong emphasis on spontaneous and fervent praise of God. This comes from the deep action

---

180 St. Teresa of Avila, *The Autobiography of St. Teresa of Avila*, translated and edited by E. Allison Peers (Garden City, New York: Doubleday, 1960), pp. 163-164.
181 St. Teresa of Avila, *The Autobiography of St. Teresa of Avila*, translated and edited by E. Allison Peers (Garden City, New York: Doubleday, 1960), pp. 163-164.
182 Teresa, *Autobiography*, p. 164.
183 Teresa, *Autobiography*, pp. 164-165.

of God within the soul. At the same time Christians can encourage one another to this style of prayer as the sisters encouraged one another in it. It is a group as well as an individual experience. For her, this jubilation was a proclamation of the reality of God among his people. The flow of praise without order and the uttering of a "thousand holy follies" sound much like the glossolalia of the present-day charismatic renewal.

St. John of the Cross

St. John was a less practical mystic than his friend Teresa. His mysticism has a more speculative note. At the same time, in sublime and poetic ways he plumbs the height and depth of mystic experience.

He refers to jubilation several times in his works. He uses the same analogy to festivity that Teresa uses. He says: "In this state of life so perfect, the soul always walks in festivity, inwardly and outwardly, and it frequently bears on its spiritual tongue a new song of great jubilation in God, a song always new, enfolded in a gladness and love arising from the knowledge the soul has of its happy state...There is no need to be amazed that the soul so frequently walks amid this joy, jubilance, fruition, and praise of God."[184]

John seems to be emphasizing the musical aspect of jubilation and makes the point that it is outward as well as inward. He goes into a beautifully poetic description of jubilation in his *Spiritual Canticle*. In highly metaphorical language John describes the Beloved (the Lord) calling to her. She then expresses to the Lord "her delightful jubilation." Like a nightingale the soul "sings a new and jubilant song together with God, who moves her to do this. He gives his voice to her, that, so united with Him, she may give it to Him...

---

184 *The Collected Works of St. John of the Cross*, translated by Kieran Kavanaugh, O.C.D. (Washington: ICS Publications, 1973), p. 609.

Since the soul rejoices in and praises God with God Himself in this union...it is a praise highly perfect and pleasing to God...This voice of jubilance, thus, is sweet both to God and to the soul."[185] Again we see in John the association with jubilation as the voice of God Himself.

Along with Crysologus and Rolle, John saw jubilation as a song that was the very voice of God. While the above passage is highly metaphorical, John may well have had in mind an outward song of the voice. Considering the use of the term "jubilation" in the mystical tradition, it is probable, though not certain, that he, like Teresa was referring to an outward jubilation. John also has a long passage in which he discusses spiritual inebriation and its effects upon the soul.[186]

St. Philip Neri

Philip Neri, who lived in the tumultuous sixteenth century, was one of the most human mystics in the history of the Church. As a layman he formed a household of laymen to help serve the many pilgrims that flocked to his native Rome.

Ordained late, he was the founder of the Oratory. He was a confessor of extraordinary warmth. Constantly joking, he loved to play games with the students in his charge. He strove to keep those around him happy and cheerful, to teach them, as he called it, in his "school of merriment."

His biographer Bacci describes this: Even when he had reached an advanced age, and his strength was nearly exhausted by his great labors, the holy man was still to be seen going about the streets of Rome with a train of young men, conversing with them on all sorts of subjects according

---

185 Kavanaugh, p. 560.

186 Kavanaugh, pp. 509-510.

to their different professions, making them affectionate one toward another and winning their reverence and love toward him... Sometimes he left his prayers and went down to sport and banter with the young men and others who flocked to him, as we learn from Cardinal Crescenzi, and by his sweetness and the allurements of his conversations to keep them cheerful and win their souls. He very often took them to some open ground and there set them playing together at ball or some other game. He could have a playful style with those in his charge, going up to people, boxing their ears, and saying, "Be merry."[187]

Philip could also feel people's sorrows. He had an amazing ability to enter into the feelings of those to whom he ministered. This empathy had a great healing effect. Bacci describes this:

> When he was called upon to be merry, he was so; if there was a demand upon his sympathy, he was equally ready. He gave the same welcome to all, caressing the poor equally with the rich, and laboring in the service of all to the utmost limits of his power.[188]

Philip's expressive style with his fellow human beings was paralleled with expressive worship toward his Lord. He constantly used his body in prayer. The intensity of his prayer would be so great at times, and he would throw himself into it in such a physical way, that he would roll on the ground. He would do this at times publicly, outside the four basilicas of Rome. Bacci describes this:

> In those places, Philip often was surprised by such an abundance of spiritual consolations, that, unable

---

[187] Bacci, *The Life of St. Philip Neri* (London: Kegan Paul, Trench Trubner and Co., 1902), vol. I. pp. 194-195.

[188] Bacci, I, p. 191.

any longer to endure so great a fire of love, he was forced to cry out, "No more, Lord, no more," and, throwing himself down, he used to roll upon the ground, not having strength to endure the vehement affection which he felt in his heart.

Bacci gives another description of Philip throwing himself on the ground:

> While he prayed he felt the incentives of divine love multiply with such power within him, and kindle such a flame in his breast, that, besides continually weeping and sighing, he was often obliged, in order to moderate the fire, to throw himself on the ground, to bare his breast, and use other means to relieve his spirit which was overpowered by the impetuosity of the flame.[189]

Philip used many gestures in his private prayer Bacci says:

> Fabrizio de'Massimi, going one morning to confession to him, found the door of his room closed, and, opening it very softly, saw the saint in the act of praying, standing up with his eyes raised to heaven and his hands uplifted, making many gestures.[190]

Philip and his friends had a warm devotion to the name of Jesus:

> Lastly, he had so tender a devotion to the most holy name of Jesus, that in pronouncing it, as he repeatedly did, he felt an unspeakable sweetness.[191] He and his friends would sing fervent hymns that called tenderly upon the name of Jesus. Bacci tells of a scene of spontaneous worship at the deathbed of a

---

189 Bacci, I, p. 19.
190 Bacci, I, p. 338.
191 Bacci, I, p. 151.

young man:

> Then in an outburst of joy, he began to sing the hymns which were sung at the Oratory, and particularly the one which begins, "Jesus! Jesus! Jesus! Let everyone call on Jesus!"[192]

Thus we see that into the sixteenth century, hymns to the name of Jesus and devotion to the name of Jesus were still very much a part of religious devotion of the period. Some of the prayer styles of Philip, especially rolling on the floor and other responses, may shock our twentieth-century religious sensibilities. Perhaps we need to remember that Philip lived in a time that was much more un-self-conscious. He desired with everything in him to give himself to God. It was only natural that he should give his whole self, his body included, over to the intensity of that desire.

OTHER MYSTICS

One finds accounts and descriptions of expressive worship, often including glossolalia style prayer, in most of the major mystics until the end of the sixteenth century and some significant accounts past this period. Let us look at some of these accounts.

St. Bernard of Clairvaux

Bernard knew an intensity of prayer that could not be contained in rational language. He says: "During these assaults of love, the soul cannot contain itself, and, to alleviate the heart, it breaks forth into expressions of love which are without order, rule or human rhetoric. It often happens, also, that the soul is mute and can merely give expressions to sighs."[193]

---

192 Bacci, I, p. 202.
193 Arintero, p. 264.

Father Hoyos

This priest gives a description similar to St. Bernard's: "Now one breaks forth in groans and tears; now one would wish to be in a desert place in order to cry out and to give vent to the vehement feelings in his breast."[194]

Fr. Juan de Jesus Maria

This Spanish writer on prayer defines jubilation:

> Sometimes a joy is felt in the interior and it surpasses all the joys of this world, and those new to the service of God break forth into outward acts of jubilation because they cannot restrain themselves. This is usually called a spiritual intoxication or inebriation.[195]

St. Alphonsus Liguori

St. Alphonsus gives his definition of jubilation on in the following way:

> Spiritual intoxication causes the soul to break forth in, as it were, delirium, such as songs, cries, immoderate weeping, leaping *et cetera*.

St. Catherine of Genoa

St. Catherine's jubilation would come out in the form of laughter. Her biographer describes it in this fashion:

> [During a serious illness] she fixed her eyes steadily on the ceiling; and for about an hour she seemed all but immovable, and spoke not, but kept laughing in a very joyous fashion... Greater interior jubilation expressed itself in merry laughter; and on the

---

194 Arintero, p. 282.
195 Arintero, p. 263.

evening of September 7 her joy appeared exteriorly in laughter which lasted, with but small interruptions, for some two hours.[196]

St. Catherine of Siena

Like Catherine of Genoa, Catherine of Siena knew laughter as a form of prayer. According to her biographer, she "was always jocund and of a happy spirit...full of laughter in the Lord, exultant and rejoicing."[197]

This doctor of the Church could also break into wordless sounds in her prayer: What then shall I say? I will do as one who is tongue- tied, and say: "Ah, Ah" for there is nought else I can say, since finite speech cannot express the affection of the soul which desires thee infinitely. [198]

St. Mary Magdalene de Pazzi

This saint would often express her fervor to her fellow nuns in a fervent manner:

> Then she was restless and could not be still. To pour out this fervor that she could no longer contain, she was forced to bestir herself and she was strangely impelled to move about. And so, at such times, one saw her moving quickly from place to place. She ran through the convent as if crazed with love, and cried in a loud voice: "Love, love, love!" ...And she said to the sisters who followed her: "You do not know, beloved sisters, that my Jesus is nothing but love, yes, mad with love. You are mad with love, my Jesus, as I have said and as I shall always say. You are very lovely and joyous, you refresh and solace, you

---

196 Baron Von Hugel, *The Mystical Element of Religion* (London: J.M. Dent and Sons), p. 13.

197 Evelyn Underhill, *Mysticism*, p. 438.

198 *St. Catherine of Siena* (New York: E.P. Dutton and Co., 1907), p. 365.

nourish and unite. You are both pain and slaking, toil and rest, life and death in one."[199]

A Fuller Reality

In the jubilation of both ordinary Christians and Christian Mystics one finds an apprehension of a wonderfully fresh and joyful reality. Jubilation was an entering to a wondrous song that came forth from the heart of God. One theme that is heard over and over again is the entering into the reality of heavenly music. Richard Rolle described heavenly music entering his ears and his heart and coming out through his voice. Medieval legends describe monks and friars being caught up in ecstasy and hearing the wondrous sound of heaven and then singing it on earth.

Dante, whose work summed up the medieval world, describes laughter and great joy in God at the heart of the Christian universe. Evelyn Underhill summarizes this view:

Moreover, the most clear-sighted among the mystics declare such joy to be an implicit reality. Thus Dante, initiated into paradise, sees the whole universe laugh with delight, as it glorifies God, and the awful countenance of Perfect Love adorned with smiles. Thus the souls of the great theologians dance to music and laughter in the heaven of the sun; the loving seraphs, in their ecstatic joy, whirl about the being of God. Thus Beatrice...so different from the world's idea of a suitable demeanor for the soul's supreme instructress, laughs as she mounts with him the ladder to the stars.[200]

Jubilation was a real entering into this delight and laughter at the heart of the universe.

Mystics were people who possessed a childlike cheerfulness,

---

199 Reinhold, *The Soul Afire*, pp. 342-343.
200 Underhill, *Mysticism*, p. 438.

a perpetual gladness of heart. Deeply in touch with the core of the universe, God himself, they shocked the world with a delicate playfulness that came from a full knowledge that they were children of a loving Father. This old medieval hymn summarizes this playful vision:

> There in heaven one hears sweet songs of birds in harmony, angels, too, sing fine melodies; Jesus leads off the dance with all the maiden host.[201]

---

201 Anna Croh Seesholtz, *Friends of God* (New York: Columbia University Press, 1933), p. 12.

CHAPTER 7

INTO THE MODERN ERA

*A large field of religious experience...
was suddenly abandoned.*
—H. Daniel Rops

As we have seen, the jubilation tradition, the tradition of expressive worship and glossolalia prayer, continued as a vital force within Western Christianity at least until the end of the sixteenth century. Yet today this tradition is almost completely forgotten. One naturally asks why this tradition diminished.

While this is an area requiring more research, there are several factors that probably played a role in the diminishing of this long tradition.

THE BREAKDOWN OF THE MEDIEVAL SYNTHESIS

As we have already seen in the chapter on the Age of Faith, the Middle Ages at its height was a time of extraordinary faith. Beginning with the fourteenth century, this remarkable Christian synthesis began to unravel. The rise of nationalism, the plague which wiped out one-third to one-half of the population of Europe within a short period of time.

In fact, much of Catholic history until Vatican II can be seen as an unraveling, a winding down of the medieval synthesis. The Protestant Reformation of the sixteenth century sent shock waves through the Catholic world. It challenged the Church to set its house in order. The Church did this at the Council of Trent but also began a move toward ever increasing rigidity. Further shock waves came with the French Revolution and the end of cultural Christianity.

Bring in Material from the Enlightenment

The scientific revolution, the growth of secular philosophy, and the loss of Church privilege all led to the development of a siege mentality, a ghetto mentality within the Church.

Though this time of the "siege" mentality was a time when one can find examples of great holiness, new orders, new inspiration, there was a growing formalism and moralism within the Church. There was a tendency to reduce the faith primarily to formulas and rules. This was not a time for rich traditions of the Church to continue and flourish.

The Breakdown of the Mystical Tradition

Mysticism, from the beginning, had been at the heart of the life of the Church. The healing and transforming power of the love of God was central to the Catholic tradition. Even the end of the Age of Faith did not mark the end of the mystical tradition; In the midst of political and theological turmoils, wave after wave of genuine and rich mystical movements preserved this vital stream of the Church's life. St. Francis de Sales, St. Teresa and the Reformed Carmelites, St. Ignatius Loyola and the Jesuits preserved this mystical tradition, enriched it and allowed God to use it for renewal of the Church.

The breaking of the mystical tradition came late. The immediate causes are easy to pinpoint—the many controversies surrounding the Quietists and the Jansenists. In the seventeenth century two opposite heretical traditions grew up—Quietism and Jansenism. Quietism replaced mysticism which emphasized extraordinary states of prayer—especially interior peace —to the neglect of active love and repentance. Extraordinary phenomena were emphasized, and immorality often accompanied Quietism.

In contrast, Jansenism emphasized the sinfulness and unworthiness of men. One Jansenist-oriented priest boasted that there had not been one unworthy communion in his church in a year. The reason was that he had not permitted any communion during the year. The pull of this frame of mind was wider than those who openly espoused Jansenism, and the effects of this mentality are with the Church until this day.

Jansenists and their fellow travelers had little use for mysticism. True mysticism for them was a rare occurrence. Unworthiness and pride would keep men from moving in a mystical direction. The Church really needed to correct the false mysticism of the Quietists. Yet in doing so, she was influenced by the Jansenist mentality, and true mystical tradition was severely damaged. Daniel-Rops describes this:

> A large field of religious experience, the whole spiritual tradition of St. Bernard, of Tauler and Suso, of St. Teresa and St. John of the Cross...was suddenly abandoned. And that loss was not without harmful effects upon the vitality of the faith.[202]

Knowledge of the mystical tradition had diminished to the

---

202 H. Daniel-Rops, *The Church in the Eighteenth Century* (London: J.M. Dent and Sons Ltd.; New York: E.P. Dutton and Co. Inc., 1964), p. 292.

point that in the eighteenth century Father de Caussade lamented:

> Prejudice and an almost absolute ignorance of mystical writers, especially of the matter contained in their works, has gradually made this name (mysticism) and its ideas so absurd that I am at a loss to describe them...

Since these wretched prejudices have prevented men from reading the true mystics of later times, it is noticeable, even in the cloister, that there has been a decrease in the number of interior souls—souls totally detached, dead to the world and to themselves.[203]

With mysticism and the strong pull of the transforming love of God de-emphasized, there more and more emerged a religion of laws, precepts, and increasing formalism. It appears that there was no direct attack on the wordless and expressive moments in prayer. Rather, the decline in jubilation was a part of the general decline in mysticism.

Continuing Traces

The experience of jubilation and the recognition of jubilation as part of the mystical tradition did not cease immediately. Rather there seems to have been a slow winding down of this style of prayer. As we have already mentioned, Gorres and other nineteenth and early twentieth-century writers were aware of the jubilation tradition. It also continued, at least to some extent, in the mystical experience of the Church until the nineteenth century.

The nineteenth-century saint, John Bosco, is said to have experienced jubilation in his prayers. His biographer states:

---

203 Pierre Pourrat, *Christian Spirituality* (Westminster, Maryland: The Newman Press, 1955), vol. IV, pp. 263-264.

When he said his prayers in common with the others, he pronounced the words "Our Father who art in heaven" with a special emphasis, and his voice was clearly heard above that of the boys on account of an harmonious vibration, an indefinable musical sound which moved all of those who heard him to tenderness and revealed that his prayer gushed forth from a heart inflamed with charity and a soul which possessed the great gift of wisdom. [204]

Catholic Culture

Catholic culture has maintained traces of the expressive worship tradition. The colorful festivities on saint's days and feasts such as Corpus Christi in Latin countries are remnants of this tradition.

Surprisingly, the idea of expressing wonder and religious emotion by wordless vocalizations is still with our culture. While writing this book I became attuned to the way wordless harmonization is used to express religious wonder in movies and in the theater. Older religious movies such as "The Song of Bernadette," "The Robe," "The Greatest Story Ever Told" and many others express moments of the miraculous or the wondrous by long periods of voices blending in wordless harmonization as background music. This is still another sign of the influence the jubilation tradition has left on our culture.

---

204 J.B. Lemoyne, S.C. *Venerable Don Bosco* (New Rochelle, New York: Salesian Press), p. 61.

CHAPTER 8

JUBILATION AND TONGUES

In God, man's weeping, and in man, gladness
—St. John of the Cross

The question arises concerning the relationship between the "tongues" of the Scripture, and the "tongues" of present-day charismatic renewal and the jubilation tradition. Are they the same experience? Is the jubilation experience the same as the experience of tongues? Is it a continuation of the tongues of the New Testament? Is it the same experience as the present-day glossolalia of the charismatic renewal?

TONGUES IN THE NEW TESTAMENT

It is not the purpose of this book to engage in biblical criticism. The issue of New Testament glossolalia has been dealt with by a number of biblical scholars. This work of the biblical scholars is well summarized in *The Gift of Tongues Today* by Malcolm Cornwell and *Baptized in the Spirit* by Josephine Ford.

In summary, biblical scholars do not see the glossolalia of the New Testament as speaking with foreign tongues but as "ecstatic utterance," a speaking forth of wordless sounds as an expression of religious sentiment.

The *Jerome Biblical Commentary* is one example of this point of view. Richard Kugelman, in his article "The First

Letter to the Corinthians" for the *Jerome Commentary*, says:

> The gift of tongues was an extraordinary manifestation of the Spirit's presence and activity (Acts 2:4-6; 10:46; 19:6). The precise nature of the gift remains obscure. Many exegetes think that it consisted of incoherent shouting; seized by a religious emotionalism under the impulse of the Spirit, a Christian would begin to shout in a fervid improvisation the praises of God.[205]

It must be added that present-day glossolalia is usually a spontaneous liturgical response rather than fervent emotionalism. Still, this description of glossolalia has much in common with Egeria's description of the Church in Jerusalem and Augustine's description of the spontaneous worship in Hippo. The tongues passages in Acts are seen as ecstatic utterance. Malcom Cornwell summarizes the opinion of biblical scholars on the matter:

> Accordingly, nearly all commentators today regard the references to tongues in Acts to be similar to the experience of the believers at Corinth. This view would provide a description of glossolalia as the utterance of unknown words or sounds as a consequence of the exuberance of a newly acquired faith of Jesus.[206]

The Fathers, however, did not see their experience as "tongues" or relate it to the New Testament experience of tongues. They were either confused by the tongues passages in the New Testament or took those passages to

---

[205] Richard Kugelman, C.P., "The First Letter to the Corinthians," *Jerome Biblical Commentary*, p. 272.

[206] Malcom Cornwell, *The Gift of Tongues Today* (Pecos: Dove Publications, 1975) p. 21.

mean speaking in languages that one had never learned.

They did, however, see a profound identity between their experience of jubilation and scriptural witness. The strongest identity for them was with the "Jubilate Deo" passages of the psalms. They felt their experience was the same as the psalmist. They likely understood the use of the word "jubilus" in the psalms as wordless singing similar to their own. Because jubilation was non-controversial and devotional, the mystical tradition saw many scriptural images of jubilation—the festivity of the father upon the return of the prodigal son, imagery of the delight of the bridegroom from the Song of Songs, imagery from Job, etc.

They also saw a profound identity between their experience and the salvation events of the New Testament. The Ascension, not Pentecost, was the time, in their view, when the apostles jubilated. Augustine records a fascinating tradition when he suggests that the apostles jubilated at the time of the Ascension of Christ into heaven:

> What, therefore is jubilation? It is a wonder following a joy that words are not able to describe. How, indeed, were the disciples filled with joy when they saw him who had been raised from the dead ascend into heaven! Words were truly inadequate to express such a joy. The joy was so great that they could but jubilate; they could but jubilate over this great joy which no one could explain.[207]

This Ascension tradition may well be the preservation in the Church of the memory of a group experience of wordless praise connected with the events of New Testament salvation history.

The question arises: "Why do the Fathers, Mothers and

---

[207] Augustine, *In Ps.* 46.

the tradition fail to connect their experience with that of tongues?" There is no clear answer to this question. Part of the reason might be that a different terminology grew up within the Church to describe glossolalia.

Accepted folk-piety often has fluid and evolving terminology. Already in the New Testament there are several terms that seem to be used synonymously to describe the experience, such as "praying with the Spirit," "blessing with the Spirit," and "singing with the Spirit" (1 Cor. 14). The Ephesian (Eph. 5:19) and Colossians (Col. 3:16) passages concerning "spiritual song" may well refer to glossolalia as well as to the sighs of Romans 8:26. Thus we see a fluid and developing terminology within the New Testament. It is also possible that other descriptive terms not used in the New Testament were applied. Perhaps other traditions and language prevailed over the use of tongues to describe the experience.

The jubilation tradition of the Church is profoundly harmonious with the view of modern biblical exegetes that New Testament glossolalia was an expression of sentiment in response to the Gospel. The Fathers and the tradition saw jubilation as wordless sounds that expressed religious sentiment also. The "sighs and groans" of the Jerusalem church as Egeria describes it were in response to the reading of the Gospel during the liturgical celebration, just as the tongues of Acts were a response to the word about Jesus. The liturgical jubilation of the first millennium of the Church came just before the reading of the Gospel during Mass and served as a preparation for the Gospel. In summary, both the glossolalia of the New Testament and the glossolalia of tradition were wordless sounds: both were a response, an entering into the Gospel in ways deeper than conceptual language.

One exciting study has just been penned by New Testament

scholar, John Poirier, *The Tongues of Angels : The Concept of Angelic Languages in Classical Jewish and Christian Texts.* He traces jubilation to second century BCE Jewish and later Christian practice of singing in the tongue of angels, the language of angels. He calls it angelglossy.

He states: "Is there a connection between the liturgical jubilus and a belief in esoteric angelic languages? Almost certainly." [208]

Paul's phrase in Thirteen Corinthians, "tongues of angels" and jubilation, both are likely, in part influenced by the tongues of the apostolic Church and the Church of the Fathers and Mothers, as well as the Medieval Church. Poirier tells us:

> By the Middle Ages – scholars have not determined exactly how early the development took place – the alleluia had been expanded by a sequence of nonsensical syllables called the "jubilus" (jubilation) which was often said to represent the sounds of angelic praise. In assessing the existence of angelglossy in the early church, we must deal with the possibility that an early form of jubilus existed in the early Christian liturgy.[209]

LINGUISTICS

Modern-day glossolalia has come under the scrutiny of linguists. One of these, *Tongues in Men and Angels* by William Samarin, delves into a linguistic study of present-day glossolalia.

According to Samarin, present-day glossolalia is not language, although it has many of the features of language.

---

208 John C. Poirier, *The Tongues of Angels: The Concept of Angelic Languages in classical Jewish and Christian Texts* (Tubingen, Mohr Sebeck, 2010), p. 141.
209 Ibid., 135.

The sounds, for the most part, are taken from the native language of the speaker. His evaluation: "When the full apparatus of linguistic science comes to bear on glossolalia, this turns out to be only a facade of language—although at times a very good one indeed."[210]

It bears close similarity to chant, mimicry, jingles, be-bop, and nonsense or baby-talk. Because of this it is similar to other created speech patterns.[211] As we have seen, Augustine and the other Fathers saw a profound identity between jubilation and the yodels and wordless sounds of the broader culture. The work of modern linguists points to the same identity with normal wordless expressions in the culture and present-day glossolalia.

JUBILATION: A CONTINUATION FROM APOSTOLIC TIMES

Indications are that jubilation is a continuation of the glossolalia of the New Testament. It is described in similar ways to the glossolalia of the New Testament as a wordless gift of improvised prayer with great spiritual significance.

Also the first references to jubilation are in the fourth century, an early date. Before this period the Church was the persecuted underground Church of the catacombs. Little is known of the daily worship and life of ordinary Christians until the fourth century. Little is known about the liturgy until this time. Thus the passing of several hundred years in explicit descriptions of glossolalia prayer should not be a surprise.

During the period of the persecutions it was generally only the extraordinary and controversial that received note. If

---

210 William J. Samarin, *Tongues of Men and of Angels* (New York: The Macmillan Co., 1972), pp. 127-128.

211 Samarin, pp. 129-149.

glossolalia prayer were not controversial and if it were an ordinary part of the fabric of Christian life, then there is little chance it would have been mentioned during this period.

Scholars of music history suggest that jubilation was a continuation of New Testament and apostolic practice. *L'encyclopedie des Musiques Sacres* suggests that it is a continuation of the glossolalia of Corinthians and the "spiritual song" of Ephesians and Colossians:

> That which concerned the Fathers, just as it had the apostles, was that one sing "in the spirit" ("with one's heart"). This is the advice St. Paul repeated to the Corinthians (1 Cor. 14:15)—"I will sing a song with the spirit"—and to the Ephesians (Eph. 5:18-19)—"Sing in the Spirit...from your fullness. Recite psalms and hymns among yourselves, and inspired songs; sing and praise the Lord with all your heart." To the Colossians he said: "Sing to God with all your heart." St. Jerome recalled this long tradition when he wrote about the jubilus, saying: "By the term jubilus we understand that which neither in words nor syllables nor letters nor speech is it possible to comprehend how much man ought to praise God."[212]

This point of view is indicated by Chambers in *Folksong—Plainsong* when he said:

> It is a life of "rapture" which the apostle looks for, quite possibly acquired through the ecstatic medium of the "jubilation." ...It may also be well to refer to the incident in Acts 16:25 when Paul and Silas, chained in prison, were "praying and singing to God," and apparently amazing phenomena followed

---

212 *L'encyclopedicdes musiques sacres*, vol. II, p. 26.

from their action.[213]

The same view is held by the *New Catholic Encyclopedia* which indicated that the jubilation of the Fathers is a continuation of New Testament and apostolic practice.[214] Biblical scholarship also suggests that plainsong and the musical parts of the liturgy emerged from the early practice of glossolalia. Werner Meyer, a German biblical scholar, states:

> The glossolalia of the early Eastern Church, as the original musical event, represents the germ cell or the original form of sung liturgical prayer. We have to think of this original music as rather simple and, seen in the light of our musical culture, as very primitive—just like everything else that is new and original; and yet, it contained all the essentials of music—rhythm, swing, the levitated flow of the tones—with a magical and enchanting grace that is quite different from anything that modern artificial weaving of the old church tones, and even in Gregorian chant to some extent, we are greeted by an element that has its profound roots in glossolalia.[215]

Thus both musical scholarship and the biblical scholarship that has dealt with the subject tend to suggest that the jubilation of the Church is an extension of the glossolalia tradition of the New Testament Church.

A Continuing Tradition

There appears to be a profound identity between the

---

213 Chambers, p. 11.

214 *New Catholic Encyclopedia* (New York: McGraw Hill Book Co., 1967): "The improvised, charismatic song associated especially with the Alleluia—continued in Christian worship"—vol. X, 105-106.

215 Werner Meyer, *Der erste Korintherbrief: Prophezei*, 1945, Vol II, 122 et seq. Translation of this quote by Arnold Bittlinger.

glossolalia of the apostolic Church, the glossolalia of the tradition and the glossolalia of the present-day charismatic renewal. There is also a very real likelihood of a medieval Catholic rooting for the glossolalia of the classical Pentecostal movement that emerged at the beginning of this century.

In the fifteen hundreds when the Protestant faith communities developed, people changed the words said in worship in theology but not their emotional and bodily response to the touches of God. Those remained the same. In Protestantism that heritage continued in early sacramental Protestant practices such as "Holy Fairs," the revivalism and camp meetings that developed into the Holiness movement and then into the Pentecostal movement of the early twentieth century. Those traditions of expressive worship grew dim among mainline Protestants and Catholics. In a sense, the Wesleyan and Holiness movement preserved as a living reality a major piece of our common or "catholic heritage."

When the Catholic Church discovered the Pentecostal movement, the Church discovered a missing piece of her own heart. The expressive worship of the medieval period and early Church was carried into the Holy Fairs.

Pentecostalism was part of the continuing wave of revivalism that began in the eighteenth century with John Wesley and with the German and continental Pietists such as Count Zinzendorf who influenced Wesley. In language, styles of prayer and emphasis on heart experience the Wesleyans and the pietists had their roots in both orthodox and heterodox medieval Catholic groups. Catholic writers such as Thomas a Kempis, Fenelon, and Madame Guyon had a profound influence on Wesley. Count Zinzendorf personally embraced the heterodox Waldensian and Hussite groups whose styles of prayer, worship, and language had medieval rootings.

Through these influences, medieval devotion to the name of Jesus, the medieval penchant for expressive worship and medieval terminology such as "spiritual inebriation" were passed on to the Wesleyan revivalists, from them to the holiness groups of the late nineteenth century, and from the holiness groups to the classical Pentecostals. Though jubilation itself was probably not preserved in fact, the climate of language, style of worship and faith expectancy that made such an experience possible were preserved. This whole area of medieval Catholic influence on Pentecostalism is an area that needs further exploration. The picture of a profound identity between New Testament, traditional and present-day glossolalia emerges. All three are a wordless vocalized entrance into the mystery of God's love. The fact that glossolalia is not usually intelligible language does not exclude the possibility that as a person yields his vocal apparatus to the movements of the Spirit, intelligible language unknown to the speaker may be produced as a sign-event of the presence of God.

CHAPTER 9

Toward the Future

The more ardently one loves, the sweeter is his jubilation.
—Richard Rolle

The glimpses we have had of the way Christians have prayed in the past are a strong confirmation of the glossolalia and expressive worship of the present-day charismatic renewal. Glossolalia prayer in a variety of forms was a basic Christian response for both groups and individuals until very late in the tradition. Improvised group jubilation was a regular part of the liturgy for nearly the entire first millennium of the Church.

Most major mystical traditions until the seventeenth century describe this form of prayer, and records of contemplatives praying in this manner can be found into the nineteenth century.

The expressive worship, so closely tied to glossolalia prayer, was also a vital part of the tradition. The existence of this tradition shows that the expressive worship and glossolalia of the present-day charismatic renewal are prayer forms profoundly harmonious with the rich tradition of Catholic spirituality.

At the same time, the tradition of expressive worship challenges charismatics to come to a new flexibility in their theological understanding of their expressive worship experience and at the same time opens them to new and better language with which to express their experience.

We are in an era that is rediscovering tradition. The legacy of the several centuries before Vatican II was one of increasing rigidity. Though the forms of this pre-Vatican II period are often called traditional, it was a period to some degree out of touch with tradition. Tradition is the memory of Jesus, the experience of the original apostolic Church finding increasing depth and resonance as the Church grows in experience.

Rich understandings of the Gospel and rich resonances of the Gospel came out hundreds of years after the New Testament was completed. The doctrine of the Trinity, the understanding of the divinity and humanity of the Lord, and Eucharistic devotion all developed in richness and depth as the Church lived out its life through the centuries. In many areas such as Scripture, spirituality and liturgy, the Church lost vital contact with its sources. The liturgical and biblical movements that led to Vatican Council II have opened the door again to tradition so that the Church can creatively face its future by drawing on the richness of its past.

The flourishing and ever-expanding charismatic movement hit the Catholic Church by surprise. This movement puts the Church in contact with forgotten sources in the mystical and spiritual tradition. In many ways, charismatic renewal parallels the liturgical renewal and the scriptural renewal. The liturgical movement involved a massive amount of research and study. The scriptural roots of the liturgy, various liturgical practices in different eras, the rich tradition of the Eastern Churches, and the experience of the Protestant churches were all sources that contributed to the renewal of the liturgy.

Yet there has been a minimal amount of going back to sources in the area of spirituality. More often than not we are filled with pre-Vatican II understandings of spirituality. In a much more significant way than in the biblical and liturgical renewals, renewal of spirituality involves experience.

It involves the experience of God, the experience of the Church and the concrete decisions to follow the Gospel. The same work of going back to sources that was done in these movements needs to be done in the area of spirituality.

Until recently the sources for charismatic renewal were the experiences of Protestant Pentecostalism superimposed upon the post-Vatican II Church. Charismatic renewal is still so new that there has been minimal incorporation of the insights of solid biblical scholarship in the renewal. There has been even less uniting with the charismatic and contemplative tradition of the Church. Charismatic renewal is a renewal of great promise to renew the Church and renew our culture. To move into its own, there needs to be a uniting with the biblical and spiritual roots of the Church.

Renewals that have profoundly shaken the Church, such as the Renaissance of the twelfth century, have involved a going back to sources. Charismatic renewal and the Church need to hear again the original stories of Francis and Bernard, of the revivals of the Middle Ages, the stories of faith powerful enough to change cultures. The original lives of the saints and the teachings of the mystics need to be heard again in our midst. In order to grow and develop, spiritual renewal needs the same going back to sources that characterized the liturgical renewal. It is going back to sources, not only with our heads, but also with our hearts.

New Understandings of Expressive Worship

Glimpses at the sources on expressive worship have much to say to our present-day experience of expressive worship.

Human Response

One of the reasons that Pentecostal glossolalia has been frightening to many is because it has appeared to be something other than a human response. The idea of "speaking in unknown tongues by the power of the Holy Spirit" is understandably a hard concept for many. The experience of the Church points to more human and natural understandings of this experience of wordless and expressive worship. As we have mentioned, the Fathers saw a profound identity between their experience of wordless vocalized prayer in jubilation and the secular yodeling and jubilation. They saw it as a basic human activity given over to a spiritual use. So today we can say that Christian glossolalia is the same human process as improvised singing in the shower, humming in the shower or yodeling. It becomes Christian prayer when this activity is given over to prayer as a means of expressing words and as a means of allowing the Holy Spirit to pray through the believer.

St. John of the Cross mentioned the gladness of jubilation as similar to the expressions of joy of a bridegroom. St. Teresa of Avila likened jubilation to the festivity of a party. Throughout the tradition, a profound identity was seen with our voices and bodies as natural to being human. A young man in love hums a new tune and does cartwheels in the park because of the joy of his new relationship.

Family get-togethers can be the occasion of much laughter and back-slapping. If you watch a group of happy people enjoying one another at a party, you are likely to see a variety of spontaneous body-gestures, laughter and happy sounds.

Likewise, sorrow and pathos are often marked by the wordless sounds of sighs, sobs and cries. In being human there are many ways we express ourselves wordlessly and expressively. Scripture and tradition present a God that is both beyond us and startlingly intimate. The greatest intimacy we know is the intimacy with God. It is natural that, even more than in daily life, spontaneous human response should be a part of that human and intimate encounter with God and with his people.

Expressive worship reinforces the Christian principle of the unity of body and soul—we are our bodies. Jubilation is also a means of groups being united on a personal level.

Just as secular wordless cries and calls unite a work crew, spontaneous harmonization deeply unites Christians in prayer. There is a group blending of spontaneity with the spontaneity of God's own Spirit.

The jubilation tradition also shows the unity of various forms of spontaneous prayer. The word jubilation came to mean a unity of wordless vocalized prayer with inspired song, laughter, tears, or body gestures. It points out that the glossolalia experience is broader than just praying aloud wordlessly. This tradition of the unity of charismatic expression is backed up by the experience of charismatic communities.

Spiritual Significance

Because the Fathers and the mystical tradition see jubilation and expressive worship as ordinary and human does not mean that they also see this form of worship as having profound spiritual significance. In fact, the spiritual significance writers such as Augustine and Rolle give to this form of worship, exceeds the importance given to it in the present-day charismatic renewal.

One recurrent theme, as we have seen, is that jubilation is the song of heaven, the song of God himself. It was a means of deeply entering into the wonder and love of God, a profound communion. Heaven was pictured as full of laughter and joyful spontaneity. The joyful spontaneity and jubilation of God's people was a reflection of the pull of the Kingdom.

Another recurrent theme has been that jubilation is a gift of prayer, a means of God praying through the person. As Augustine said, "God himself turns the tune." Contemplatives have always contended that the richest prayer is prayer without words, prayer that God himself gives as a gift. Jubilation is an entering into God's gift of prayer with voices and bodies as well as hearts.

The tradition beautifully blends the human and spiritual sides of expressive prayer. The Mass is both startlingly ordinary and at the same time a means of encountering the risen Christ in his totality. Jubilation is also ordinary and, at the same time, a rich means of encountering God.

A New Conceptual Framework

The tradition of jubilation and other forms of expressive prayer gives a new conceptual framework for understanding glossolalia and expressive prayer. Because this form of prayer is ordinary and human, much of the misplaced fear and misunderstanding concerning glossolalia can be alleviated. The identity with yodeling, humming and other ordinary human activities helps to overcome this fear that "tongues" is a mysterious supernatural "happening."

Terms such as jubilation, free style harmonization, sounds of wonder, and Christian yodeling can be used alongside standard pentecostal terminology for glossolalia. Such terms indicate the broader conceptual base that tradition gives to the experience of glossolalia and reinforce the human and ordinary nature of this form of prayer.

Jubilation and the Liturgy

The proper home for jubilation is in a liturgical setting. As we have seen, expressive worship was tied to the liturgy and liturgical celebrations such as the Divine Office. The alleluia-jubilus which was improvised until the ninth century by congregations was a standard preparation for the reading of the Gospel.

Personal Prayer

Jubilation has strong implications for personal prayer. Because it is a means of God praying through the believer it is a means for more people to experience the gift of contemplative prayer. It is a "teacher" of prayer, as Cassiodorus put it. The tradition can also open Christians up to "mystical jubilation," the spiritual drunkenness that results in rich expressions of joy.

The tradition of the saints, mystics and doctors of the Church can open up Christians to laughter, tears and all sorts of expressive body motions in their personal prayer. It is also important to note that jubilation is simply one style of prayer. Silence, liturgical prayer, and rote prayer such as the rosary are equally important and should all be integrated into a healthy prayer life.

The Broader Context

Expressive worship is not the goal of the Christian faith. The birth of the Kingdom through a response to the Gospel is the goal of the faith. Expressive worship is simply one part of a much broader whole.

Charismatic renewal has been a great gift to the Church, a "stream of grace" as Cardinal Suenens puts it. It is an important part of the spiritual renewal of the Church. Renewed experience of the Spirit, the gifts of the Spirit and community are coming through the charismatic renewal.

Any renewal however, faces the danger of myopia, of looking inward to the areas that are its special emphasis. The broader Church needs to be renewed by the charismatic element, but the charismatic element also needs to be renewed by the Church. A healthy listening to tradition, the biblical and liturgical renewals and other renewals within the Church can call the charismatic renewal to transcend itself, to grow out of itself and more truly become the gift to the Church it is meant to be.

The Church is being challenged by the poor and starving of the world to both hear and live the Gospel in radical ways. Expressive worship has a role to play in a more total renewal by making these realities personal and visible and by being a means to celebrate these realities with one another and with God.

Conclusion

People yearn for God. It is as though our hearts hear, even if faintly, a sound everlasting in its origin whose beauty bids us, "come close and listen." You see signs for this spiritual quest everywhere. Within Christianity (Protestant, Catholic and Orthodox) I see a hunger for the recovery of a rich, human and grounded spirituality. You can find Baptists learning contemplative prayer and Catholics influenced by Pentecostalism, Pentecostals appreciating liturgy. Secular culture also is on a quest. Meditation, yoga, and generic spirituality hold many in their sway.

In this atmosphere quick spiritual fads can blaze up and then die quickly for lack of fuel. Where do we turn? To be rooted, we can turn to what my cousin Dhyani calls the voices of our ancestors.

The song, the sound we long to hear, is a sound of wonder. We ache to see this earth, which we have commandeered and shrunk with our technology and industries, afresh through a lens of amazement. In short, we want the everyday sights, sounds and events of life to astonish us and to again dance to the ineffable music of a God who can saturate our lives, and even, I pray, our culture.

What we long for, even though indistinctly heard, is the song of Christ, reverberating in the Scriptures, Church tradition and in the development of different Christian faith communities. You see ancient spiritual writings newly translated and made available for reading.

We are on a quest for things nearly forgotten.

As we have seen in this book so far, we are, as is stated in Hebrews, surrounded by a great cloud of witnesses; first of all in Scripture and then in the spiritual writings of our 2000 year history as Christians.

Part of what we want is a faith that is down-to-earth, human, approachable, yet at the same time one that can listen in on eternal music of a cosmos, created and animated through Christ.

A big missing piece of this puzzle has been jubilation and expressive worship. For most of Church history, jubilation and expressive worship were at the heart of faith life. When God touched people, it affected them body, soul and emotions. The whole of their being heard the eternal song and went through the catharsis of transformation through the cleansing power of the Holy Spirit.

In the past, people have responded to that eternal song in awe of silence, in the cleansing of tears, in the jubilation that joins our vocal sounds to the rhythm of that eternal Godly song.

Jubilation as defined and depicted by all the witnesses in this book often sounds like the experience of modern Pentecostal churches and charismatics of many faith persuasions. And, as some significant scholars suggest this all goes back to the glossolalia in the New Testament described by Paul.

Yet there are hints that the jubilation tradition drew on rich resources just now beginning to be tapped by modern Pentecostals and charismatics.

We all can see much further when we stand on giants' shoulders, no matter how short we may be ourselves. The jubilation tradition unfolds the story of many giants whose shoulders we can climb.

The jubilation tradition came about in a time when Christianity was both powerful and tender, powerful and tender enough to change a culture.

We find in our ancestors in faith a raw openness to the Spirit that attracted millions and turned the world upside down. Great Cathedrals like Chartres developed from common people caught up in the Spirit and gifts of the Spirit. Great hymns and prayers grew from all this. The jubilation/glossolalia heritage gave birth to plainsong and, perhaps even, the whole of Western music.

Giant figures like Thomas Aquinas, Augustine, Ambrose, Catherine of Siena and Teresa of Avila and hundreds of others opened themselves to the wondrous, the miraculous, and in their persons touched people with the touch of God as they sang their songs of jubilation. They lived in cultures imbued by the wondrous.

Several things stand out that we can learn from. They saturated themselves in Scripture, often praying, like Francis, ten hours at a time. These figures, and so many others, formed a harp that the breath of the Spirit turned into a melodious song that entranced the world.

The poor were especially close to the heart of so many of these giants. They embraced a Christianity with a preferential option for the poor.

We need that type of renewal today. And signs show that renewal is arriving on the breath of the Spirit.

On June 19, 2009, Pope Francis, then Cardinal Bergoglio, dropped to his knees at a convention of 5,000 Protestant and charismatic evangelicals and asked that hands be laid on him for strengthening and blessing.

This openness to learning from different Christian

traditions is vital. Christians of the different faith traditions need each other to be whole.

It is one thing to read a book about jubilation. It is another to encounter this wondrous heritage personally along with brothers and sisters in Christ.

When Catholics look on Pentecostalism they see more than a Protestant faith tradition different from their own, they have an open experiential current example of how their own ancestors of faith prayed, a window on how their Church prayed for 1700 years.

These ancestors in faith have much wisdom to share with us, wisdom that can remake our lives and our churches. May we listen to their voices.

Contact the Author

You can email the author of this book at this address – pmissions@charter.net

Parish Missions and Retreats

The author of this book, Deacon Eddie Ensley, along with Deacon Robert Herrmann, offers parish missions, retreats, and conferences throughout the country. A mission by the two deacons draws the whole parish together. It recharges the congregation. Everyone takes time for the important things like wonder, mystery and prayer. People reconcile. Faith is awakened. Vocations are discovered. Families are healed, lives are forever changed. The parish discovers afresh its ultimate calling and meaning.

To bring one of their retreats or missions to your parish or area, you can contact Deacon Ensley at pmissions@charter.net or visit his Website: www.parishmission.net